No Time To Die
A Holocaust Survivor's Story

This book is a history documentation, presented in the form of a witness account and dedicated to my grandchildren, David, Rebecca and Joseph.

Karl-Georg Roessler

Cataloguing in Publication Data (Canada)

Roessler, Karl-Georg, 1923-

   No Time to die : a Holocaust survivor's story

   Autobiography.
   Includes bibliographical references.

   ISBN 1-55207-009-3

      1. Roessler, Karl-Georg, 1923- . 2. Holocaust, Jewish (1939-1945) - Personal narratives. 3. Theresienstadt (Concentration camp). 4. France - History - German occupation, 1940-1945. 5. Jews - Germany - Biography. 6. Holocaust survivors - Biography. I. Title.

DS135.C97R63 1998   940.53'18'092   C98-940112-5

Karl-Georg Roessler

No Time To Die

A Holocaust Survivor's Story

Robert Davies Multimedia
MONTRÉAL—TORONTO—PARIS

Copyright © 1998, Karl-Georg Roessler
ISBN 1-55207-009-3

Robert Davies Multimedia Publishing Inc.,
330-4999 Saint-Catherine Street,
Westmount, Quebec, Canada H3Z 1T3
☎ 1-800-481-2440 / 1-514-481-2440 📠 1-888-RDAVIES
e-mail: rdppub@netcom.ca

Distributed in Canada by General Distribution Services
☎ 1-800-387-0141 / 1-800-387-0172 📠 1-416-445-5967;

in the U.S.A.,
from General Distribution Services,
Suite 202, 85 River Rock Drive, Buffalo, NY 14287
☎ 1-800-805-1083
or from Ingram Book Company

In the U.K. from Lavis Marketing (Oxford)

For all other countries, please order from publisher
e-mail: mail@rdppub.com or rdppub@netcom.ca

Visit our Internet website:
http://www.rdppub.com

The publisher takes this opportunity to thank the Canada Council and the Ministère de la Culture du Québec (Sodec) for their continuing support of our publishing.

"For thou shalt forget thy misery; thou shalt remember it as waters that are passed away; and thy life shall be clearer than the noonday; though there by darkness, it shall be as the morning. And thou shalt be secure, because there is hope."

Job 11: 16-18

Acknowledgements

I wish to acknowledge my debt to my friends and helpers, who read early drafts of my manuscript and gave their valuable comments. Moreover, I am deeply grateful to my wife, Friedl, for her untiring patience. Only with the support of all involved could I finally complete this book.

Karl-Georg Roessler

Introduction

One may ask what prompted me to write about experiences during Hitler's reign in Europe. Although given in a different context, I find the words of Deuteronomy 4:9 very fitting:

"But take utmost care and watch yourself scrupulously, so that you do not forget the things that you saw with your own eyes and so that they do not fade from your mind as long as you live. And make them known to your children and children's children."

Yet, keep in mind that what is written here did not only happen to me, but, in similar ways, to millions of Jewish people; mothers, fathers, old people, those in the middle of their life expectancy, teenagers, small children and infants. And worse, most of them did not even survive. They were murdered by various methods — by being shot, gassed, beaten to death, hung or starved. In fact, approximately six million Jews did not survive. Neither did millions of non-Jews. Do you realize that six million means roughly twice the total Jewish population of the State of Israel?

Much knowledge about these past events has already been buried under the gravel, sand and mud of time.

But let us first clear the basic facts. I come from a mixed marriage. On my mother's side, the family was Jewish, although assimilated into Western liberalism; my father came from Christian background. After what I had experienced during the "Thousand Year Reich", I knew where I belonged. Although I was Jewish by matrilineal descent anyway, after thorough studies, I decided to adopt the Jewish faith.

Part One

1. KLEIN-OMI

My grandmother was the embodiment of kindness and goodness, as well as being a patient and always interested listener. Her personality and her appearance radiated a natural dignity, and she was one of the best things that ever happened to me. I might say she was "aristocratic", but I do not like this term, because it might indicate some snobbishness, behaviour which she certainly never displayed.

She was of average height and very slender, with a kind face surrounded by white hair which was parted in the middle. When I was seven years old, she was seventy-one. Her face had deep wrinkles, which sometimes accentuated her expression of worry. She had met with hard times.

She came from a very wealthy family in Warsaw, married a well-to-do banker in Germany, and things went quite smoothly for years. Then came World War I. Two of her sons, both decorated with the Iron Cross medal, were killed on the battlefield. Her husband had died of a heart problem. When the war ended, her money was gone, and so was her family's. They had invested heavily in government war bonds ("I gave Gold for Iron!"), but now the bond documents were not even worth enough to heat a room for a few minutes. Then came the terrible inflation which ate up the rest of her savings.

From a twelve-room apartment in Hamburg's finest residential district, she moved to my hometown, a small town in Saxony. She rented a three-room flat on the third floor of an apartment building on King Frederic Augustus Street, and was supported financially by her only surviving son and her son-in-law, who was my father. Later, when times became even harder, she had to move to a still smaller flat, which had only a kitchen/living room and a bedroom. I like to remember the times when we visited her on the King Frederic Augustus Street, where she had beautiful pieces of black mahogany furniture in her living/dining room. In her bedroom she had an exquisitely hand carved dresser with a secret compartment in which she kept her personal papers. This, of course, was very exciting for me as a boy.

As long as I can remember my grandmother, whom we called Klein-Omi (Little Granny), was dressed all in black. But what made her appearance special, and why she was so well known in our town, was her headgear. After so many years it is difficult to recollect the exact construction of it. It must have been a wire structure covered with black tulle cloth, and with a short veil hanging down the back to approximately one inch below her neck. Nowadays, one would think this thing looked funny, and indeed it was unusual even in her days. One could almost have believed there was a big black bird with very short wings and a veil-like tail sitting on her head.

It was mostly on Sundays that she visited us. When she began having problems with walking, we picked her up by car. Like many people from Eastern Europe, she had a harsh accent; nonetheless, she spoke fluently not only Polish and German, but also French. We children played games with her and were usually faster at grabbing things (for instance with the Prepare-Hopp card game), since her hands were shaking all the time with the palsy of old age. Not very much, but enough to prevent her from having full control of her grip. On these occasions she always had dinner with us, and while we all enjoyed a sweet dessert, she had a slice of dark farmer's bread with salt on it. She preferred this to any cake or compote.

A few years later, her arthritis began to bother her a lot. Joints and bones were aching, and she had to use a cane when walking. But nobody ever heard her complain. In spite of her warmth, she was always somewhat reserved and kept problems to herself.

She was well-liked by the people of our town. Once a labourer fell from a scaffolding next to the house in which she lived. She immediately asked his co-workers to bring the man into her apartment and put him on the couch, while she phoned the doctor. While waiting for the physician to come, she put cold compresses on the man's head, gave him juice and watched him carefully. Much later, when the last of her personal effects had been confiscated and were being auctioned off by the Gestapo, this man bought one of her paintings — which was all he could afford — hoping to return it to her later. Of course this was not possible, because she never returned to our town, nor indeed to any other place. She was killed at the age of 83. This man's family still has the painting as a meaningful reminder of what had been.

On one occasion, much later, after I had been away with my sister for a short mountain-climbing holiday in the Austria mountains, I visited my grandmother who had by then already been transported by the Gestapo to a ghetto house in another city. She and her fellow-lodger listened with great interest to my stories, moving the openings of their ear-trumpets as close as possible to my mouth. Hearing aids, as we know them now, did not exist. It was very depressing for her to live, for the first time, in cramped quarters with somebody else. Being reserved, she liked her privacy. In fact, neither of these elderly ladies were used to sharing cooking facilities, bedroom and table with anyone but their families. But Mrs. Selma Simon was a nice person. Nazi government regulations required that she, like all female Jews, had to add "Sara" to her name. So we called her "SSS" for short, but only among ourselves.

My sister and I loved Little Omi dearly. This was why I undertook such a hazardous enterprise as voluntarily entering the Theresienstadt (Terezín) Concentration Camp in April 1943; I simply wanted to keep a promise and see my grandmother.

II. NAZI LEGISLATION
(ANTI-JEWISH DECREES)

Nazi government policy, politics and state laws provided the administrative foundation for the destruction of European Jewry. While legal matters may be sort of dry to read, they, nevertheless, give a basic understanding of the circumstances under which Jews already had to live, in the early years of Nazi-Germany. One cannot grasp all the implications of this oppressive system, or the atmosphere of horror it created among Jews, without knowing at least the most fundamental anti-Semitic decrees enacted during that time.

After the monarchistic regime of the Kaiser and the lost war (World War I), democracy was a transplant which did not work in the way it was intended to do. In 1933, Hitler came to power in Germany. He had a bag full of election promises designed to take advantage of both the German mentality of nationalism and obedience to an authoritarian head of state and the country's poor economic situation with its high unemployment and depression. People were looking for a hero, a strong man, who would lead them out of the disaster. With Hitler, Germany got another autocratic ruler. He and his followers were prepared to annihilate the Jews. But even though Hitler's book, "Mein Kampf", was a script for the Jewish tragedy which was to follow, hardly anyone took the book or Hitler's rhetoric seriously.

Democracy in Germany at that time had been quite unstable. Governments came and went, but none of them had been able to get the poor economy and unemployment under control.

At one point, many Germans thought that they should try Hitler: maybe he could do something. In the trend towards right and ultra-right parties, the democratic governments lost their majority.

Two different reactions combined played into Hitler's hands. On one side were people who genuinely wanted to try him out, and on the other side were people who felt that letting Hitler take over as chancellor was the only way to prove that he was unable to improve the situation. Both sides voted for him; hence the majority.

Many considered Hitler a parvenu, a social climber, and believed his anti-Semitism could be dealt with in a democracy. After all, to live in an anti-Semitic atmosphere had been a way of life for Jews in Europe for centuries. Even the Catholic Church had often stirred up their people against the Jews, as had Martin Luther, the founder of Protestantism, who wrote several anti-Jewish treatises, including a most vicious one entitled "On the Jews and their Lies." But the world had not yet seen the likes of what was to come.

When the Nazi party got a majority in the 1933 election, Hitler became Chancellor. He was now in charge of the government, and this meant authority. Obedience to authority was bred into the German character. Hitler used this to his advantage by stating that the only way he could get the economic situation and all of its bad side effects under control would be for him to have parliament's consent to act quickly and singly, i.e. without parliament's explicit permission for each decision. This was actually meant for emergency cases only, but, later, it was only Hitler himself who determined what was an emergency, and what was to be done about it.

At that time, people were ready to go out on a limb in order to try everything possible to fight poverty, hunger and starvation in the country. And so the Reichstag (the German parliament) approved the Enabling Act, which gave Hitler all the power he needed to do whatever he wanted to do, without parliamentary approval. To get enough yes-votes, the Nazis, in their insidious scheming, officially called the Act "Law for the Elimination of Need from People and Reich." Many deputies thought nothing could be wrong with voting for a law to improve the economic situation.

With a law backing him up, as well as having the police, the army, his political hordes, the SA (Storm Troopers), the SS ("Defense Corps of the Führer"), and all of his buddies in the right places, Hitler started a relentless fight against his political opponents. People were virtually beaten into obedience. Step by step, the laws which protected the rights of the people were changed or removed. And so the Enabling Act turned democracy into a dictatorship. The first concentration camp was built, and there began a reign of terror.

I can understand that it is not easy for people who grow up in a peaceful country to understand all of this, but try to imagine what would happen if protective laws no longer existed. Gangs, supported by a gangster-chief, break into your house, destroy the contents, beat up your parents, and take your father away, and nobody knows where he is. He winds up in a concentration camp where people are kept without heat, with hardly any food, and sometimes have to stand in rain and snow until they collapse. Some are beaten and some are hanged for even the slightest transgression concerning camp rules. There is no health care, of course, but there is hard labour every day.

You cannot go to the police, because they work together with the government under a dictator. You have no right to go to court and complain about the terrible injustice which has been done to your family. In fact, under Hitler, hoodlums invaded the courts, seized lawyers and judges, and dragged them through the streets. Well, all these things really did happen to thousands upon thousands of families in Germany.

Hitler wanted to get rid of the Jews. Why he developed such a pathological hatred of the Jews has been much discussed by medical and historical authorities, but we will never really know. The fact remains that he never, personally, suffered any harm from any Jew. He was a lunatic and a fanatic, but, unfortunately, these characteristics were not very obvious at the beginning of his leadership.

Not only were laws changed or removed, but many new ones were promulgated. Included among such laws, as they came into existence in Germany throughout these years, were the following:

— The "Law for the Restoration of the Professional Civil Service". It not only prevented Jews from finding employment within the civil service, but also removed those already there. †Hundreds of university professors and lecturers were hurt by this. At the same time, Jewish lawyers were either expelled from, or denied admission to, the bar.

— Another law denied Jewish students admission to universities or other institutes of learning.

— Government departments were no longer permitted to employ Jews.

— Jews were expelled from all positions which involved contact with the public, such as the press, radio and movie industries. Television did not exist at that time. Even in the fields of art, such as theatre, literature, music, and painting, Jews were no longer permitted to perform.

— Jews who had been, or had become, German citizens lost their citizenship, and with it not only their right to vote, own land, etc., but eventually also their right to continue living in the country. They were Subjects without civil rights.

— Jewish farmers could no longer bequeath their children what they owned. They lost their properties.

— One of the corner stones of anti-Jewish Nazi policy were the so-called Nuremberg Laws. The full name was "Law for the Protection of German Blood and German Honour". This law determined who was considered either a Jew or partly Jewish, as viewed by the Nazis. Only Germans or "persons of kindred blood" could be citizens. Jews could not. Jews were not permitted to marry non-Jewish Germans, or even live with them. Germany, as many European countries, had a system of police registration. No matter where one lived in Germany, one had to report to, and register with the local police authorities. Unless one went underground (which happened mostly just before, or during, World War II), the police, state security, SS

Crimmitschauer Anzeiger und Tageblatt

Nr. 267 — Crimmitschau, Freitag, 15. November 1935 — 87. Jahrgang

Der gesetzliche Schutz deutschen Blutes und deutscher Ehre

Die erste Verordnung zum Reichsbürgergesetz und die erste Verordnung zur Ausführung des Gesetzes zum Schutze des deutschen Blutes und der deutschen Ehre — Dr. Goebbels zur Jahrestagung der Reichskulturkammer — Aufruf General Görings für den Luftschutz — Die Parlamentsdebatten in England

Die 1. Verordnung zum Reichsbürgergesetz

1. Verordnung zur Ausführung des Gesetzes zum Schutze des deutschen Blutes und deutscher Ehre

Publication of Anti-Jewish Decrees in German local press, 1935 and others could easily ascertain one's whereabouts. Since only relatively few people succeeded in going into hiding, the Gestapo (Secret State Police) usually got whomever they were seeking.

Here are some more examples of anti-Jewish Nazi laws:

— With the Reich Citizenship Law, Jews were deprived of all remaining rights, such as access to legal authorities and social services.

— Jews had to report the possession of all money over the equivalent of $5,000. Police stations and Revenue offices had lists of addresses of Jews. If a Jew owned a company, he had to mention the fact that he was Jewish to the authorities. This applied even to those Jews who had converted to Catholicism or Protestantism. According to the Nuremberg Laws, any person with three or four Jewish grandparents, or any person of the Jewish faith, was considered to be a full Jew. Other religious affiliations were not considered.

— Jewish physicians were not allowed to treat non-Jewish patients and had no access to hospitals. Jewish lawyers could no longer practice law.

— Each Jew had to send an application to the authorities requesting the addition of a Jewish name (Israel for men and Sara for women) to all their documents and identification papers. By so doing, they could easily be identified as Jews. One must bear in mind that in Germany everyone who left his house had to have identification papers on him at all times. Identification passes for Jews were imprinted with a big "J ". This constant publication of new decrees and a little bit of hope in-between that things might get better as time went on, caused my mother to compare this situation with a construction ram. Going up (hope): tak-tak-tak, and coming heavily down (new decree): bang.

In 1938, many Jews were deported from Germany to a narrow strip of no man's land between the borders of Germany and Poland. It was bare land: there were no houses which could provide shelter against the cold, and no kitchens in which they could prepare food. Germany had expelled them, and Poland did not want to take them in. Such deportees, exposed to the weather

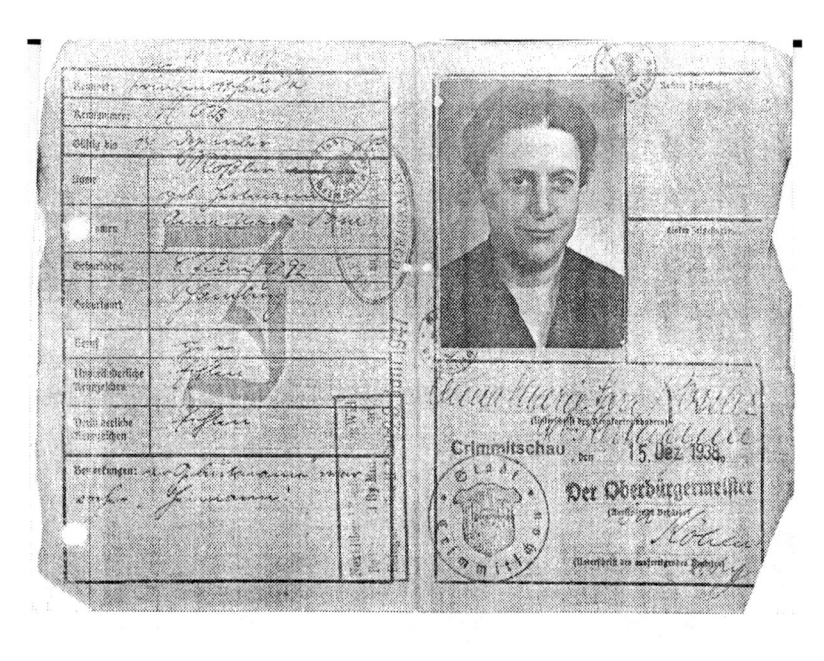

German identification card for Jews

day and night, stayed there until the Poles finally accepted them. One angry and desperate boy, Hershel Grynszpan, the cousin of a late friend of ours, whose parents had been treated in this way, shot a German embassy official in Paris. This was just the moment for which the Nazis had been waiting. They secretly mobilized their SA and SS hoodlum gangs, and during the night of November 9th, 1938, under the eyes of the police, all hell broke loose. A pogrom took place all across Germany. Over two hundred synagogues were set on fire and destroyed. Windows of Jewish stores and homes were broken. Shops were looted. Dwellings were demolished. Jews were beaten, arrested, incarcerated, and many even killed.

This night was called Kristallnacht (Crystal Night, or Night of the Broken Glass). Wherever Jews lived, there was broken plate glass littered all over. The Gestapo watched and reported back most carefully to their Reich Security Headquarters. The Jews themselves had to pay the German government one billion marks for the damage the SA and SS had done to Jewish property. The amount demanded, in today's terms, was roughly equivalent to one billion dollars. If the fact that the Jews had to pay for the damage done to them does not seem logical — That's right, it is not. If this does not appear to be just — it is not. If everything looks twisted... **it is.**

From that time on, it was illegal for German Jews to own gold, silver or jewels of any kind. Other restrictions followed.

— All Jewish enterprises now had to close. A Jew could no longer own a business. Some Germans were able to make a fortune on these transactions by buying whatever Jews possessed at distressed prices. Their purchases were worth five or even ten times the amount Germans paid for Jewish property. The same principle applied when Germans took over Jewish dwellings. By being in the right place at the right time, non-Jews could get flats and houses for peanuts. Other Germans who owed money to Jews could simply default on their debts, and Jews could not claim their rightful money in any court.

— Jews were not allowed to go to movies, theatres or concerts, or even sit on public park benches.

— Jews could neither own nor drive a car.

— Jewish dentists, pharmacists and veterinarians were no longer allowed to practice.

— Even before this, Jews could not own land. Now they could not even rent flats or houses. The state confiscated Jewish houses and crowded many families into what were called "Jew-Houses", or "Ghetto-Houses". Members of these families were restricted to limited outdoor hours. They were allowed outside only between 6:00 a.m. and 8:00 or 9:00 p.m., and could not leave the city, town or village in which they were living without having a special permission from the Gestapo.

— Radios, bicycles, cameras, binoculars, typewriters, microscopes, pianos and other musical instruments had to be given up and delivered to the police.

— Jews were not allowed to use public transportation, such as streetcars, busses, trains, or taxis.

— As of September 1st, 1941, every Jew had to wear a yellow Star of David with the inscription "JUDE" (Jew) on his or her outer garment. Jewish dwelling places also had to be marked.

This should suffice to explain how Jews became total pariahs. They were expelled, evicted and isolated by the German government and its functionaries, and exposed to grossly highhanded actions. Socially, they were not permitted to keep contact with their former non-Jewish friends, who in turn were threatened with punishment if they maintained their relationships. Sometimes these threats were enough to scare away even non-Jewish relatives. When someone once said to the head of the SS, H. Himmler, that he knew a very respectable Jew, Himmler snapped at him with sarcasm: "Every German has his 'decent' Jew!".

In short, Jews were sitting ducks, readily identifiable and easy to apprehend and transport into concentration camps where they would most likely be killed. There was even an official Nazi song with the lyrical content "...when Jewish blood spurts from the knife, things will go well...".

Once all this has been fully grasped, it will not be difficult to understand the circumstances under which all of the following happened.

One incident occurred when I was fifteen or sixteen years old. The Gestapo was a secret but very powerful organization within the state. As serious as this incident could have become, looking back, the whole thing became a comedy in which the Gestapo made complete asses of themselves.

My father had a friend in East Prussia, who had been his superior officer in World War I. He owned a printing plant and a manorial estate there and my parents had sent me to him for a four-week summer vacation. In Königsberg, East Prussia, where he lived most of the time, I spent many hours around the stables and riding his horse. His son had been drafted into the army, but I saw him when he was on leave. During sight-seeing tours I took pictures with my cheap camera, in the synagogue and from the roof of "Uncle" Bruno's house, and also made notes of the times the boats left for harbour tours. In fact, I made many notes, including whenever someone called and I had to give a message to "Uncle" Bruno. There was one, for instance, from a colonel whose name I do not remember. I also marked down the housekeeper's macaroni recipe, which I had liked especially well.

One day I made a trip to a spit of land between the sea and a bay, and lost my wallet there. However, I did not realize this until the day before taking the train back home, when I was looking for my ticket and could not find it. "Uncle" Bruno bought me a new ticket, but the wallet was gone.

Back at home, we got a call from the Gestapo in the district capital summoning my father and me to appear at their offices. First they talked to my father without me, and then they sent him out of the room and called me in. To hear the name Gestapo scared everyone out of his shirt. To have to go in there for an interrogation left me gasping for breath. The wallet had been found and brought to the police, who in turn had given it to the Gestapo, because they believed it was the key to spy activities. The photos of the outside and inside of a synagogue were extremely suspicious to them, and so were the pictures taken of the city from the roof. They were sure the macaroni recipe and the timetable of the harbour tours were secret codes. They had put the Colonel, "Uncle" Bruno and his son for a long time under constant surveillance, and also bugged their telephones.

In the end, the Gestapo returned my wallet and the train ticket. The other contents were kept in their files, just in case... I am sure our family was shadowed for quite some time, too.

Why was the Gestapo at beach resorts in East Prussia? Admiral Wilhelm Canaris was commander-in-chief of the counter-espionage of the German armed services. In 1935, Canaris agreed to give the Gestapo the authority for counter-espionage within the borders of the German Reich.

In my spare time I took piano lessons and played a lot of classical music, until our grand piano was confiscated. Then I played whenever and wherever I could, mostly light music and by ear.

I was in the last year of high school. Originally, I had planned to study medicine, but people of Jewish origin were no longer admitted to universities or other schools of higher learning. Then, before I could pass my final examination, another new law came into force which meant that I was fired from school.

III.
THE BEGINNING OF THE WAR
— THE GHETTO HOUSES —

For reasons too complicated to explain here, and without direct relevance to this context, my mother and father divorced. Thus, my mother became the one in the most dangerous position because, although certainly she had never denied being Jewish, the fact that she was married to a Gentile had given her some measure of protection. That protection was now gone. She therefore applied for immigration visas for the United States and Britain. Her application number for the former was 76113, but at that time we did not realize that being so low down on the waiting list meant that she did not have a chance in the world getting out of Germany.

On the morning of September 1st, 1939, my mother got up to prepare breakfast. I had expected a specially warm hug and kiss when she came into my bedroom to wake me up, because it was my birthday, but instead she said with a very sad voice that Germany had invaded Poland. And so, only twenty years after the last World War ended, a new one had started. She must have realized the implications, namely that there would be no way now to get out of Germany and away from Nazi terror.

In the cold of a November morning in 1941, my uncle Otto (my mother's brother), who lived in Hamburg, was picked up and deported to the then German-occupied Soviet city of Minsk. He and other Jews were taken there in unheated cattle cars. Later, the SS took truckloads of Jews, and pressed them into air-tight vans which had been camouflaged as caravans (trailer homes). They closed the doors and connected hoses which led the exhaust fumes from the engine into the vans. Then they drove several kilometres. It took ten to fifteen minutes for the poisonous exhaust gases to suffocate all the prisoners in these vans.

Detailed descriptions of how these poor bodies looked when a burial crew pulled them out of the trucks was given in testimony during the trials at the International Military Tribunal in Nuremberg. The dead prisoners were covered with all kinds of excretions, such as faeces, urine, and vomit. Blood had come out of their eyes, ears, noses and mouths. This was done to thousands of Jewish prisoners. My uncle was just one of them. [1] [2] [3] [4]

Suspecting that his deportation was imminent, my uncle had left his signet-ring with friends to be given to me. This ring has become one of my most cherished possessions, and I wear it at all times.

Being told of my Onkel Otto's deportation, was how my beloved grandmother got knowledge of the end of the last of her three sons.

In 1941, Little-Omi was told by the Gestapo that she had to move to Plauen, a city south of us, into a Jew-House, or Ghetto-House, as it was called. With the exception of some clothes, bedding and a few essentials like pots and some dishes, everything she owned was confiscated by the Gestapo. The document said: "Based on paragraph 1 of the Law concerning the confiscation of Communist property, dated May 26th, 1933 ....in connection with the Law regarding the confiscation of property of enemies of the people and the state, ...and in connection with the decree of the Führer and Reich-Chancellor of May 29th, 1941, ...the total property of the Jewess Laura Sara, widowed Hertmann, nee Bergson, living at ...., is confiscated herewith, and will be auctioned. This is in accordance with the mayor and the Secret State Police ....concerning the dissolution of Jewish households."

My dear, dear grandmother. She had nothing to do with communism, and categorizing her as an enemy of the state and

Nr. 3/42 des Geschäftsbuches

Abschrift.

Versteigerungs-Auftrag

Die unterzeichnete Auftraggeberin

Laura Sara verw. Hertmann geb. Bergson in Crimmitschau, Albertstr.15,

erteilt hierdurch dem unterzeichneten vereidigten und öffentlich bestellten Versteigerer

Alfred Trätner in Crimmitschau, Carolastraße 4,

den Auftrag, die in anliegender Liste unter laufender Nr. 1 bis 31 enthaltenen Sachen zu versteigern.

Die Versteigerung soll am 29. April 1942 ab 9 Uhr in Crimmitschau,
Albertstraße 15, stattfinden.

Der Auftraggeber ist Eigentümer der genannten Sachen.

Die Sachen sind gebraucht -

Anlaß der Versteigerung:

Die Versteigerung erfolgt auf Veranlassung des Oberbürgermeisters zu Crimmitschau, bezw. der geheimen Staatspolizei zu Chemnitz, Dienststelle Plauen, betr. die Auflösung von jüdischen Haushaltungen.

Die Sachen befinden sich in Crimmitschau, Albertstraße 15.

Order for confiscation of Jewish property (Klein-Omi)

people was ridiculous. How can one visualize a kind-hearted eighty-two year-old woman, who could hardly walk anymore, as "an enemy of the people"?

She moved in with Mrs. Simon (SSS), as previously mentioned. [5]

A year later, my mother was deported to the same city. Her property, too, had been confiscated, since she was also classified as an "enemy of the people and the state". Together with other families, she had to move into an empty factory. Because there were no separating walls, they hung blankets on ropes to provide family units with at least a minimum of privacy.

After Mrs. Simon had been deported to the Theresienstadt Concentration Camp, my grandmother was moved to the same factory building, so that she could live with my mother. The building, a back-house, which could be reached from the street only by using a passage, was in bad shape. Plaster had come off the walls, bare bricks showed, and windows were defective. The concrete floors were cold. Since a makeshift kitchen had to be used by several families, a schedule was established showing who could use the kitchen, and at what time.

The street-level apartment of the house through which one had to go in order to get to the back-house was occupied by a staunch Nazi, whose job it was to check on who was coming and going. He also had to lock and open the gate at the passage at the times determined by the Gestapo.

Most Jews had already been deported from the city, either directly to extermination camps in Eastern Europe or to Theresienstadt (Terezín), which was called "a Ghetto for the Privileged." But as with all Nazi propaganda, this was also one big lie. In reality, Theresienstadt was only a stopping point for most of the Jews who were then transported to Auschwitz and their death.

There were people from all walks of life in the Ghetto Houses of Plauen, former merchants, factory owners, salesmen, store owners, a cantor from a burnt-down synagogue, an accountant, etc.

By law, only Jewish physicians were permitted to treat Jews. But since there were no more Jewish doctors left in the city, real problems arose. One lady was suffering severe pain caused by advanced cancer. Finally, the Gestapo permitted one German physician to treat Jews. Dr. Niemeyer — may his memory be blessed — was the angel of the sick Jews. He was not only a physician but what we Jews call a "mensch", a good, kind, helpful and sympathetic person. Later, when Jews were actually prohibited from getting medical help at all, he still continued to treat Jews and to give the dying lady narcotics to ease her pain. Nevertheless, she had to go on a "transport". "To go on a transport" was the common designation by Jews for a deportation transport to a concentration camp.

One could not phone the doctor, not even in an emergency, because Jews were neither permitted to own a telephone nor to use a public one. One had to go halfway through the city to get in touch with Dr. Niemeyer, and could do so only during the times when Jews were permitted to be outdoors.

There were always new "transports" leaving and always more suffering. Eventually everyone who lived in the Ghetto Houses shared in the tragedy of losing parents, brothers and sisters, other relatives or friends.

My turn came in 1943. I moved in with my mother and Klein-Omi. Because I was the child of an intermarriage, I did not have to wear a yellow Star of David, which meant that I could do many things the others could not do. While other inhabitants were allowed to go only to specified stores, and were readily identifiable because their food ration stamps were red and marked with a "J", I could go practically unnoticed to all stores and at least try to get some extra food. On the other hand, I was considered a Jew, because I had sided with my mother in the divorce case of my parents. "He shows the Jewish blood," they said.

Not only did Nazi-Germany want to get rid of Jews as fast as possible for political and ideological reasons, but also because food was in short supply, and Jews were considered "unnützige

Fresser" (useless eaters).

Our standard supply consisted of potatoes, cabbage and dark bread. With the J-rations one did not get milk, butter, eggs, cheese, meat, fowl, fish, white bread, cake, honey, fruits, preserves, tobacco, or any of the special allotments which the Germans got from time to time. Things like chocolate and real coffee or tea were completely out of our reach.

Jews who had originally lived in Plauen sometimes managed to get some extra food from stores where they had been customers in normal times. People like my mother, Klein-Omi and I, who had been moved to this city by order of the Gestapo, had little chance of getting anything without ration stamps. Only seldom did I succeed in getting some fish here, a few vegetables there, or maybe some fruit once a year. Lacking butter, cheese, sausage, jam or other things one could spread on bread, my mother fried some onions in a little paraffin oil I had been able to lay my hands on, mixed them with a paste made from flour and water and created a bread spread.

When the Allied bombing raids on German cities increased, Jews were not permitted to take refuge in general air raid shelters. They had to remain completely unprotected in the streets or houses.

Jews were banned from public streets on which government or party buildings were located. They were not allowed in public parks or to use park benches. Jews who used public rest rooms or bathing institutions were arrested.

Jews had to carry their documents with them at all times, not only to prove their identity, but also residence and work place, if any.

I could go on and on describing the subhuman conditions under which Jews had to live in those days. All this was done, to quote Nazi jargon, "to separate Jews from the 'body' of the German people".

IV.
MY GRANDMOTHER
AND THERESIENSTADT (TEREZÍN)

Klein-Omi could hardly walk from one chair to another anymore. Not even with her cane. One day, in the cold February of 1942, the Gestapo came with a van, and drove right to the back building in which we lived. Ten people were ordered to pack, what they felt was essential, within twenty minutes. They were allowed to take only as much as they could carry, and not more than two pieces of luggage. Klein-Omi could not carry anything, but she was finally permitted to take a suitcase and a bed-roll which I then carried downstairs for her, and other prisoners. Three people, including me, had to carry her in a chair down three flights of stairs to the van.

I found out that she was taken to a cell in the city hall, and then did all I could do to get permission to visit her. Finally, I went to the Gestapo and was lucky enough to get a visiting permit for myself, but, unfortunately not one for my mother.

It was one of the most heart-rending moments in my life. There, in a cold, humid and dark prison cell, on a foul smelling mattress which was lying on the cold stone floor, was my dear grandmother. Outside, in the corridor, prostitutes were chatting and giggling. She did not complain, even in this demeaning situation, but showed her typical, venerable, matriarchal composure. Kneeling beside Klein-Omi, I broke down and sobbed. I loved her so deeply. But it was she who comforted me. After a while a policeman came and said my visiting time was over.

Message about Klein-Omi's death

Knowing that my speciality was chemistry and pharmaceuticals, she asked me in a plain sort of way if I had anything with me to give her. It was clear to me that she wanted something to end her life. As cold as it may appear, I am grateful to this day that I did not carry anything of that nature with me. What a burden on my conscience either way! I solemnly promised that I would do everything humanly possible to see her again. The next day Klein-Omi was on her way to the Theresienstadt Concentration Camp.

In the fall of 1942, a lady living in the same building as we did, received a short note from a gentleman who was transported to Terezín together with my grandmother (He was later gassed in Auschwitz). Mr. Perl, the last head of the Jewish Community Plauen, wrote, among other things:

"...Mother Hertmann passed away on April 7th..."

However, this information came to me only many months after my daring venture to visit my grandmother.

The Gestapo put an end to my practical work as a pharmaceutical assistant, which was meant to be a preparation for future studies. I was fired from Alte Apotheke (The Old Apothecary), and could not readily find another job, because everybody was scared to hire someone of Jewish origin. Finally I succeeded in getting employment with a textile company engaged in the preparation of hemp and flax bast fibres, because they needed somebody qualified to set up their laboratory.

The plant manager was not afraid to hire me. He had a fairly high position in the Nazi workers' union, but was otherwise anything but a Nazi.

One day in March 1942, he told me that there was going to be an instruction course on bast fibres at the Technical College in Prague, and I was to attend. The official and euphemistic Nazi word for occupied Czechoslovakia at the time was Protektorat. To enter the Protektorate one had to have a special permit from the local Gestapo. Because the manager of my company knew well that I would never get such a permit, he requested a document from the local police and had it also signed and stamped there, as well as by the city, and the employment authorities. All three of them trusted him implicitly, because of his rank. With this paper in my pocket, I went on my way.

The train stopped at the border and SS-men checked for the correct permits. When they saw my documents, they immediately asked me to take my suitcase and get off the train. Hoping to hide the strange feeling in my stomach, I stressed that everything had been arranged by my employers, who obviously had not been properly informed on whom they should have approached in order to get the correct permit. Moreover, I pointed out the fact that the lectures would begin the next morning, that I had been registered, and my boss expected me to be present.

The train was ready to depart, and I was the only obstacle. The SS-men finally turned a blind eye to this irregularity and let me go on the train.

My Visit to Theresienstadt (Terezín)

My return was set for April 8th or 9th. I had my return ticket, and Professor Sch. handed me my border permit, which he had obtained through the administration office of the Technical College. They had answered the questions printed on the permit form:

Jew? Half-Jew? with NO. I wonder what would have happened if they had asked me to answer.

At one point on the return journey, the express train stopped, and I heard the conductor call out: "Bauschowitz/Theresienstadt". It did not take long for this surprise to sink in. Although such a stop-over was not expected, let alone planned by me, I quickly grabbed my luggage and got off the train, remembering well that promise given to my grandmother, so deeply engraved on my mind.

In one of the houses near the train station, I asked the Czech people where I could leave my suitcase. Of course, they asked me where I wanted to go. Since they had impressed me as being reliable, I told them about my intention to go into the concentration camp. They were stunned at the thought of such an undertaking and tried to talk me out of it. They cautioned me because of the risks involved. But since I remained stubborn, they agreed to keep my suitcase, and wished me luck. From then on, I had nothing on my mind but my dear grandmother, and how happy she would be that her grandson had kept his promise in spite of all the adversities which beset us. The last days of her life would be filled with the joyous thought that I had visited her. I learned only months later that she had died before my attempt to see her.

With an official-looking leather briefcase under my arm, I started walking along the road to Theresienstadt, noticing that it was one of those typically grey early spring days. The snow had gone, but nothing was green yet. Everything around that road was muddy, and had a dirty-brown cast. As if this was not depressing enough, the road lead through a graveyard. It was cold, but I probably also felt chilly from the uncertainty of what would happen to me. On the right side, in a shallow valley, a crew of Jews guarded by SS-men worked in the fields: a dreary view of slowly moving, dark, bent figures, with many large black birds — crows or ravens — cawing overhead.

The memory of this macabre scene has never left me. It always triggers a permanent association of black birds with death.

A horse-drawn wagon with Jews under guard passed me. They drove toward the train station, probably to pick up some goods or mail for the SS: who knows? I passed a German Air Force hospital on my right, and then came to a fork in the road. As far as I can remember, the road to the left went to Leitmeritz, and the one to the right to Prague. Another road branched off half to the right, and I could see a turnpike and a guardhouse.

With the briefcase under my arm, like an official on business, I asked the SS-guard to direct me to the KZ-commandant (KZ is an abbreviation for the German word concentration camp). To my surprise, he did not ask any questions, but just told me to bring an exit pass on my way out. He said: "go straight along the street to the market place where you will find the commandant's office". Without having to show him any identification, I was able to walk around the barricade and on as directed.

Theresienstadt (Terezïn) was an old Bohemian town, with equally old fortifications which were ideal not only for defence in times past, but also for isolating inhabitants.

Incidentally, the Serb terrorist, Gavrillo Princip, who started World War I by assassinating Archduke Franz Ferdinand, heir to the Austrian throne, died here in 1918, imprisoned in the fortress.

The Germans occupied Czechoslovakia in 1939. In 1941, the former inhabitants of Terezïn had to move out of the town, which was then converted into a concentration camp. The nineteenth-century military barracks lent themselves to becoming mass shelters.

I passed ramparts and casemates and reached a little park-like area through which a group of Jews came, all wearing the yellow star. Seeing a chance to get first-hand information, I stopped and waited until they came close. As soon as they saw me, the men took off their caps and the women bowed, which appeared very strange to me. All of them seemed to be very uneasy. I wished them good day. This prompted one man, who made himself the spokesman of the group, to point out that they were not permitted to speak to Aryans without being asked to do so. "What Aryan?" I said, "I am of Jewish descent myself," and I went on explaining to them that I was here to see my beloved grandmother. They threw their hands up, said, "Heaven forbid", and scurried away.

Moving on, I reached a part of the street which was separated from the houses by wooden partitions. From one of the houses I heard terrible screams. Three years later, I learned from my mother that this was the home for the elderly, deranged and incurables, and that conditions there were absolutely horrible. The people in this home were completely helpless, half-starved and old. Lack of space and people to provide personal care contributed to this Dantesque place of torment.

Mrs. Simon (SSS) died here.[5]

There was a gap in the wooden fence, and a Jewish guard stood right beside it. He wore a black peaked cap with a yellow ribbon around it, had insignia of rank, an official number and a belt made of white canvas. When I spoke to him, he snapped to attention thinking I was a German Aryan. The man was astonished at my impudence in entering the KZ and doubted very much that I would ever get permission to speak to my grandmother. When I inquired about the general situation and conditions, he answered that what was happening in Theresienstadt could not be described with simple words. A report on the facts would fill many volumes. If and when the regime ever ended, it would be up to the survivors to give an account.

SS-headquarters was located in the middle of one of the streets forming the market square. My heart was beating very fast when I entered this building. On the ground floor to the left was a room with Czech policemen whom I asked to see the Commandant. Dr. Adler wrote in his book, "Theresienstadt",[6] that one could find among the Czech gendarmes some evil characters who were absolutely on a par with the SS. But the majority were not, and some even helped on occasion, if provided with substantial reciprocal services.

When I explained why I was there, they looked first at each other, then at me, and then proceeded to very strongly try to dissuade me from pressing my luck any further. They even hinted that it was very risky to approach SS-Hauptsturmführer Siegfried Seidl [7] with such a demand. But again I insisted. One of them led me up to the next floor, into a room where a uniformed SS-man sat in front of a typewriter. Again, I asked to see the Commandant in order to request permission to visit my grandmother. He hesitated, but to refuse my wish and let me leave the KZ seemed to exceed his competence. He opened the door to the adjacent room, and announced me to his boss.

All of a sudden I no longer felt very courageous. I had

reached the top of the ladder and realized that, most likely, I would take a serious fall. Not only did this man have the power to refuse my demand, he also had the power either to have me shot on the spot, or to let me disappear without trial or any other legal formality. He was the highest authority in the Theresienstadt Concentration Camp, and nobody would ever know my whereabouts. I tried to be smart, to make a good impression and to let Seidl know that my visit to the KZ was known on the outside. Standing at attention, I requested in a short military manner his permission to see my grandmother.

SS-Hauptsturmführer Seidl, in his black uniform with skull-and-crossbone insignias, seemed to be puzzled for a moment. He did not look mean or cruel, and a ray of hope crept into my mind. But I was wrong. Seidl suddenly bursted into a scream at the top of his voice. His face contorted, he yelled that it was absolutely audacious to walk into the ghetto camp, and, above all, to ask to visit a grandmother! I tried to stay calm and replied very politely that I had not entered the ghetto by illegal means and certainly realized that he had both the right and the power to decline my request, but that I had made a promise. Another outburst followed, after which I merely asked him to please give me an exit pass. Seidl seemed to spit fire. He screamed that I should go to hell. He would not give me a pass.

Realizing that there was nothing more I could do, I left Seidl's office. I implored the SS-adjutant for a pass, but he just shrugged his shoulders and said that there was nothing he could do. I felt as if all the blood had run out of my body, and I was nearly paralyzed with fear. I walked down the stairs, out of the building, and through the streets in a daze. Soon I reached the guardhouse. Although I tried to look very nonchalant, the guard made sure that I could not escape, and then called headquarters on the phone. They told him not to let me out.

As Eugen Kogon confirmed[8], the SS also committed many persons with only two Jewish grandparents to concentration camps.

Not only had I become a witness of the inside of a concentration camp, but also a prisoner. Moreover, for all practical purposes, I did not even exist anymore, because I was an *unregistered* prisoner. Trying to persuade the sentry was useless, because he just followed orders from the KZ-boss. Any attempt to escape through the turnpike would be fatal: the sentry would shoot without hesitation. Even believing that my grandmother was there did not help. In fact, I did not know anyone in the camp, which then held over 45,000 prisoners. And, of course, I was not at all familiar with the layout of the ghetto camp.

In my perplexity, I walked back to the ramparts and casemates which extended right and left from the road. In a moat-like strip beside, or quasi-between, the casemates, was a swamp.

Behind the swamp and up on a sort of dam-like slope I saw Jews working on a cheval-de-frise type barbed-wire fence, while a guard (a Czech gendarme) walked to and fro, but at a considerable distance. I tucked up my trouser-legs and stepped carefully into the swamp. Covered by a casemate wall, I moved cautiously towards the work crew until I came to a corner. Had I gone any farther, I would have been in full view of everybody, including the guard. At this point, I must have been twenty-five to thirty meters away from the fence.

When the guard turned to walk away from the crew, I managed to give a hand signal, waving someone to come to me. A rather tall and broadly-built man rushed up to me when the guard made his new turn away from us. In a few words, I explained to him how I had come into the camp, why I simply had to make a break for it, and asked him to please open the wire fence just a little bit, so that I could slip through. It was not at all clear to me just what I was asking of them, and what could have happened to them as a result of agreeing to help me.

The guard turned, the man rushed back to his fellow-inmates and talked to them in a very low voice. I saw them, as one after the other shook his head or shrugged his shoulders. With hope almost abandoned, I nonetheless tried to emphasize my desperate situation by gesticulating silently. Whenever the guard turned to face in my direction, I hid behind the wall at the corner.

Then, suddenly, I noticed that the large barbed-wire frame had been moved a fraction, and there was a small gap in the fence. I waited for the right moment when the guard had just turned away from the crew, then started running. Up the slope, through the gap in the fence, across the field, running, running. I ran with all my strength and must have been completely out of my senses, numb, and did not know — and still do not — whether there was any shouting or shooting. I ran until I collapsed from exhaustion at a wall on the far side of the Air Force hospital. I felt as though both my heart and my head would burst. My lungs hurt and my chest felt as if it were tied tightly with a rope. When I had halfway recovered, I made my way with great caution back towards Bohusovice (Bauschowitz) and the train station.

But first, I met up again with the people who had kept my suitcase. They greeted me, then dried and cleaned my shoes, socks and trousers. They served hot tea, while I told them in detail what happened and, of course, our discussion was not without their comments of "we told you so". The next express train to Dresden was scheduled to leave after dark, so before then they made sure that there was no search party out looking for me.

Returning into German Reich Territory, fortunately, went without a hitch. When I finally arrived in Plauen, however, it was well after midnight, and as I said before, we were not allowed to be outside after 8:OO p.m. I knew that the gates of the passageway would be closed and controlled by the loyal Nazi in the front building, so I had to climb over a lath fence, onto a garage roof, over a wall and into the yard of the factory building which had been converted into our Ghetto House. By that time everybody was asleep. I could not make much noise, because the rear bedroom windows of the front building also bordered on the yard. By throwing small stones against a window, I succeeded in waking Mrs. Hofmann, and then had to convince her in a whisper to keep her voice down. Very soon everybody in the house who was not bedridden met in our cubicle and heard my story.

To this day, I still do not know who, or how many of the people present, believed my story that night. My mother did not, as she admitted to me many years later. She had found everything too fantastic to be real, as though it were taken from a movie or novel. Later, when she was "introduced" to Theresienstadt and saw everything for herself exactly the way I had described it — the market square, the ramparts and casemates, the uniforms of the Jewish ghetto police and the Czech gendarmes, etc. — she remembered her doubts and told me that her conscience had really bothered her about this.

V. MY MOTHER AND THERESIENSTADT (TEREZÍN)

The few Jews left in the Plauen Ghetto Houses gradually became even fewer, and, in January 1944, my mother and about twenty others were ordered to pack up and leave. Only two of them survived and returned after the Liberation, my mother and one gentleman. From all that could be found out, these two were saved by a clerk's registration error. The others all went on another "transport" and were gassed in Auschwitz.

My mother's orders came on January 8th, 1944, while I was working in a laboratory. As usual, I went "home" during my lunch hour to see my mother. I found our living quarters sealed. A lady who was in the house told me what had happened. She had not been allowed to notify me. Shortly after I had left for work that morning, the Gestapo had come and told my mother and the others to prepare two parcels or suitcases with the most essential things, but not more than each could carry. Again, they had had to be ready within twenty minutes. Meanwhile, the Gestapo had been watching everyone. It had been a replay of the orders given when my grandmother had been taken earlier.

First, I rushed to friends and phoned my sister[9], who took the next train to Plauen. Then I made inquiries as to my mother's whereabouts. It turned out that the twenty-two people from our building and other Ghetto Houses in the city had been taken to the city prison. Next, I went to Gestapo headquarters and requested permission for my sister and me to see our mother. This was refused twice, with the explanation that the man in charge was not in. But I did not give up so easily. The third time I asked, permission was granted. In the meantime, my sister had arrived. I filled a little bottle with a certain solution and put a label on it, and then we hurried to the prison to be there before nightfall.

With a female prison guard present, we were allowed to speak with our mother, separated by a long table. All three of us tried to remain very restrained. My mother said that, unless she met with a violent death, we should rest assured that she would stick it out and see us again. At this point the guard broke down in tears. She sobbed and said that never before had she had to guard such innocent people, and that she felt like an accessory to a crime. Although prison regulations required strict separation of prisoners from visitors, she pushed the table away to let us embrace our mother. She also said that we could give our mother anything we wanted, even though this was absolutely against orders. She was not willing to burden her conscience any more than she had had to do already.

What I had put into the little bottle was diluted hydrochloric acid, which I had tested weeks before, to make sure that it was weak enough to be used as invisible ink. If one held the paper over a flame or other heat source, the writing would appear. The label said "Stomach Drops", and gave instructions as to their use. I believe I wrote something like "four or five drops in a glass of water", knowing that such a dilution would not harm anyone, even if one had to actually drink it as "prescribed." I told my mother that, if somebody asked, she should say that she had to use the diluted drops for her "subacid gastritis." Thanks to the friendly prison guard, I could then instruct her on how to use the solution for writing. How this worked for us will be explained later.

When all was said, we embraced for one last time, and none of us could hold back the tears. My sister and I well knew that this could have been the last time we would see our mother alive, and my mother could hardly help but fear that she would never see her children again.

The Nazis had many techniques by which they could rob the Jews of their last possessions. It is ridiculous to pretend that

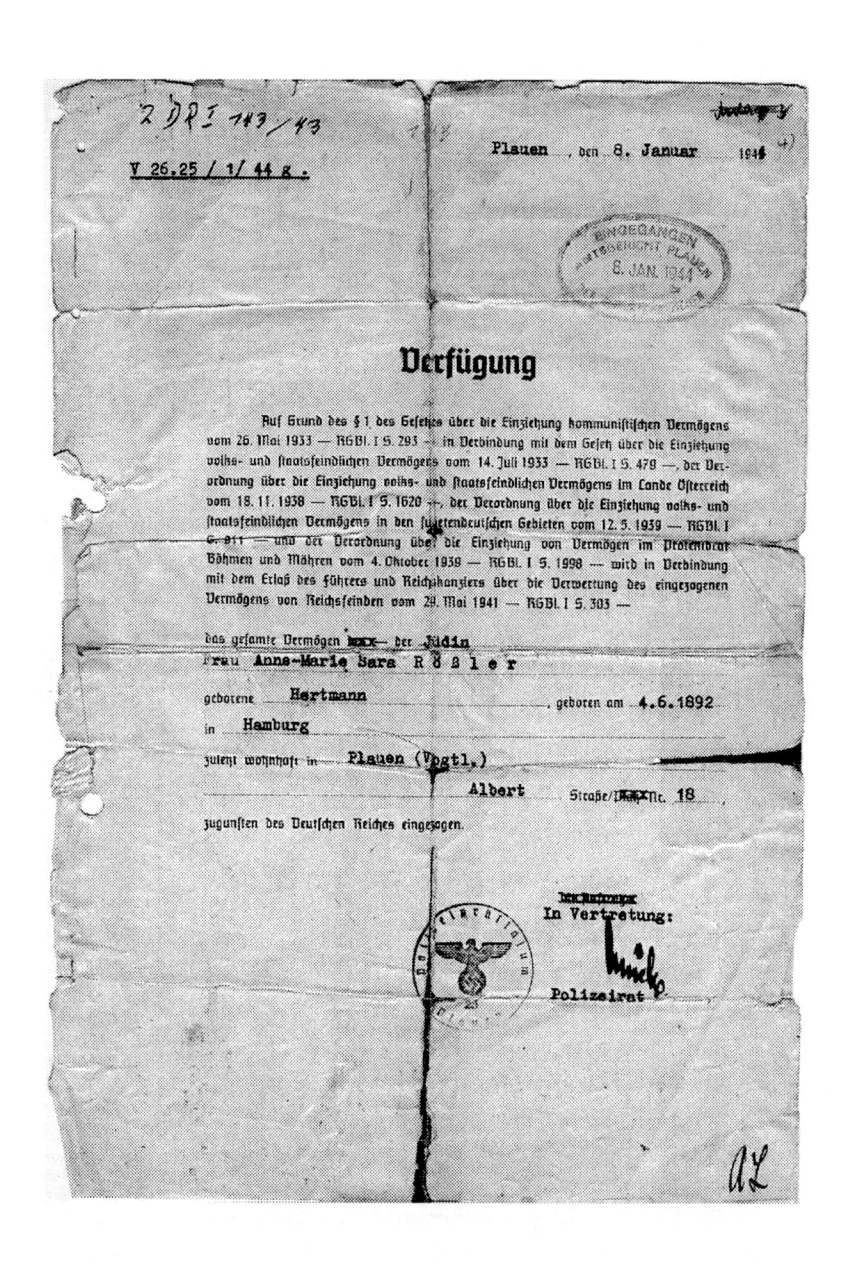

Z DR I 143/43

V 26.25 / 1/ 44 g.

Plauen, den 8. Januar 1944

EINGEGANGEN
AMTSGERICHT PLAUEN
8. JAN 1944

Verfügung

Auf Grund des § 1 des Gesetzes über die Einziehung kommunistischen Vermögens vom 26. Mai 1933 — RGBl. I S. 293 — in Verbindung mit dem Gesetz über die Einziehung volks- und staatsfeindlichen Vermögens vom 14. Juli 1933 — RGBl. I S. 479 —, der Verordnung über die Einziehung volks- und staatsfeindlichen Vermögens im Lande Österreich vom 18. 11. 1938 — RGBl. I S. 1620 —, der Verordnung über die Einziehung volks- und staatsfeindlichen Vermögens in den sudetendeutschen Gebieten vom 12. 5. 1939 — RGBl. I S. 911 — und der Verordnung über die Einziehung von Vermögen im Protektorat Böhmen und Mähren vom 4. Oktober 1939 — RGBl. I S. 1998 — wird in Verbindung mit dem Erlaß des Führers und Reichskanzlers über die Verwertung des eingezogenen Vermögens von Reichsfeinden vom 29. Mai 1941 — RGBl. I S. 303 —

das gesamte Vermögen der Jüdin
Frau Anna-Marie Sara Rößler

geborene Hartmann, geboren am 4.6.1892

in Hamburg

zuletzt wohnhaft in Plauen (Vogtl.)

Albert Straße/Platz Nr. 18

zugunsten des Deutschen Reiches eingezogen.

In Vertretung:
Polizeirat

Notification regarding confiscation of author's mother's property

the Gestapo was the only part of the German administrative apparatus responsible for the suffering of the Jews. No, every part of the government was involved in these despicable actions. After the rooms or flats were locked and sealed by the Gestapo, the judicial system took over and cleaned everything out.

Yes, the courts themselves helped the Nazis, with pseudo-legal papers.

Keeping Jews in city prisons before transporting them to a concentration camp served two main purposes: to prevent them from escaping or committing suicide, and to have them prepare lists of their possessions being left behind, such as household goods, furniture, clothing, even down to postage stamps. Before living quarters were sealed, the Gestapo searched everything from top to bottom for hidden jewellery, concealed documents or proof of still-existing bank accounts. Rent, gas, electricity and water had to be paid up by Jews up to the day of the transport. In many cases, Jews had to pay even for their own transportation to the concentration camp. Food, coal and soap ration stamps had to be handed over to the authorities.

Another scheme, documented and described by Adler [6], was the swindle with "home purchase contracts". Jews were made to believe they could acquire the right to own a home at whatever destination had been chosen for them, and that they could pay for this from their blocked bank accounts. Little did these people know that in most cases their final living room would be a gas chamber.

Theresienstadt was said by the Nazis to be a model ghetto for privileged Jews. Among those said to be deported to this "Paradise Ghetto" were German Jews who had been soldiers during the First World War of 1914-1918, especially officers and those seriously disabled ex-servicemen, who had had arm or leg amputations. But all this talk was just to mislead both Jews and non-Jews about the real situation. This deception found its peak in the Verschönerungsaktion (Beautification Project) which will be dealt with later.

Of all the Jews who were deported to Theresienstadt, only

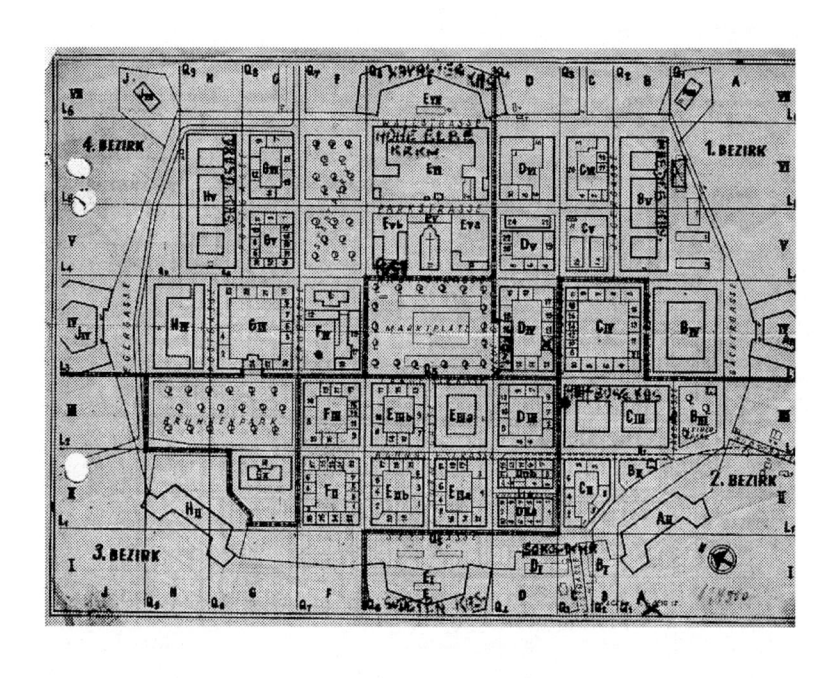

Map of Theresienstadt (Terezín) concentration camp

a small percentage survived. The majority was merely in transit, and they were later either gassed in Auschwitz, or died of hunger, sickness and deprivation. Before Hitler shot himself, he urged the Germans to continue the killing of the Jews, and even bragged about the massacre of the Jews.

My mother's "transport" was designated as V/10. It went from Plauen to Dresden, and on to Theresienstadt, arriving there on January 11th, 1944. Her "transport" number was 429. An SS-"transport" detachment and a Gestapo escort controlled the prisoners on the train.

Arriving Jews were first led into the Schleuse (the sluice). It meant that they were channelled through a temporary holding place, which could be described as a filter, where baggage was searched and all sorts of things taken away, such as money, medication, and valuables which were possibly hidden, or even toothpaste, hair tonics, skin creams and tea. A lot of these items were stolen by the searchers who worked for the SS.

As mentioned earlier, Theresienstadt, situated on the river Ohre (Eger), used to be a pleasant old Bohemian town called Terezín in Czech. About five thousand people lived there before being ordered to evacuate by the Nazis in 1941. Close to fifty thousand people were crammed within its walls when it was turned into a ghetto. In its northeastern corner was the infamous Kleine Festung (Little Fortress). This was the prison, punishment, torture and killing facility for the Jews of Theresienstadt. Fourteen Czech gendarmes were also executed there in October 1943 because they had helped Jews. Anyone taken into the Little Fortress could not expect to leave it alive. It took a miracle to escape from this tightly guarded fortress. Yet, there were two such escapees lined up with me in the penitentiary in 1945 to be shot. Again, by a miracle they were lucky to survive, and so was I. Fate had intervened. But that is yet another story.

At the time my mother arrived in Theresienstadt in January 1944, the bestial SS-Obersturmführer, Anton Burger, who had formerly been a teacher, was camp commandant. He had succeeded Siegfried Seidl in July 1943. In February 1944, came his successor, the former mechanic, SS-Obersturmführer Karl Rahm. Whenever they or their subordinates appeared in their black uniforms, the inmates tried to avoid them. Depending on the mood they were in, one could easily be punished or even executed, like the old man who did not pull his cap from his head fast enough, when an SS-man approached. The Czech gendarmes and the Jewish guards, whom I mentioned earlier, were also part of the control mechanism of this concentration camp.

Theresienstadt now had ten times the normal number of people living there. Therefore, the buildings, mostly barracks, were filled up to the lofts with sleeping places, mostly two-story bunk beds. Such an overfilling could only lead to unsanitary conditions. There was no place which was not vermin-infested. Rats, as well as an indescribable stench, came from the sewers. Decomposing garbage also contributed to the general contamination problems. The lower stories had restricted water-use periods because of a general shortage, and things were considerably worse on the upper floors, where there was hardly any water pressure.

The health situation was particularly bad for the old and weak ones. Because of the lack of food and heating, they easily caught colds, which resulted in pneumonia and then death. Many Jews were already sick and weak when they were transported to Theresienstadt (Terezín).

There was always a shortage of nurses, and even those who were there sometimes stole from the already insufficient food supply for the destitute. This brings the weak and sick Klein-Omi to my mind. What she must have suffered in her last weeks!

At all hours, carriages were being pulled by people who removed the dead.

1. — In the Theresienstadt Camp -

This table shows what a prisoner was supposed to receive each day in the summer of 1943:

FOOD PRODUCT	WEIGHT	EQUIVALENT
Meat:	35.7 g	1/2 hot-dog
Flour	71.4 g	8 tablespoons
Sugar	28.6 g	2 1/3 tablespoons
Margarine	26.8 g	Not quite 1 1/2 tablespoon
Potato	357.0 g	3 medium— sized potatoes
Bread	375.0 g	Slightly more than 12 ozs.
Jam	14.3 g	Slightly over 1 tablespoon (if available)

Later (1944 to 1945) there were no vegetables for the average inmate.

Almost everyone got his food from big kettles located in a large kitchen. For the average Jew there were no individual rations. All inmates, but especially those who worked, were always very hungry. However, so much was stolen that inmates actually received only a fraction of the official rations mentioned above. This meant hunger, becoming half-starved and weaker every day.

Certainly, quite a bit of the foodstuff wound up on the black market and was exchanged for other not readily available items. Onions and garlic were highly desirable food adjuncts because of their vitamin content and their flavour-enhancing properties. They had a high black market value.

Depending on the SS-commander, and other not-readily-identifiable circumstances, inmates were sometimes allowed to write a limited number of cards, e.g. once in three months. Only thirty printed words, including salutation and signature, were permitted, and on one side of the card only. Inmates were not

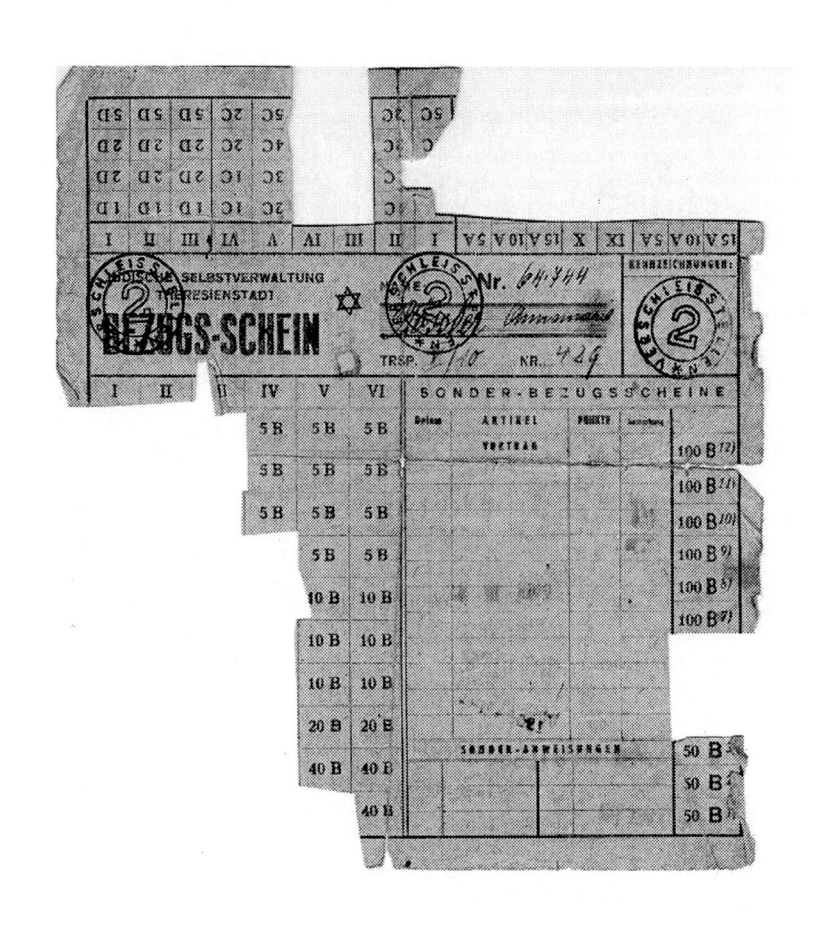

Example of ration tickets at Theresienstadt concentration camp

allowed to mention names of people inside or outside the camp or to ask for parcels or any specific items. These cards, so important for the inmates, were then censored to make sure they did not contain any information about living conditions in the concentration camp. Even with, or because of, all these controls, thousands of cards never reached their destination. They were just left lying around, got lost or were somehow destroyed.

There were also regulations by which a deportee was permitted to receive some post-cards and very few parcels each year. The rules for post-cards from outside were essentially the same as for the ones leaving Theresienstadt — thirty printed or typewritten words on one side only, and no more than one card at a time. Parcels or their contents, in kind or weight, could not be mentioned. Picture post-cards were forbidden, and many other restrictions applied.

The number of parcels that could be sent again depended on special regulations and also on the area from which they were sent, such as Greater Germany or occupied countries. One could not send any food item which Jews living outside were not allowed to get on their J-rations, like chocolate, real coffee, or tobacco. Such things were immediately confiscated in the camp. A parcel would also be confiscated if it contained any written notes. Many parcels were stolen at the postal control stations, but we were lucky in that my mother received almost all the ones my sister was able to send — and with the original contents intact. In fact, even little things like medication, which my sister hid in carefully resealed cardboard boxes of ersatz coffee, arrived untouched, although the packages always had to pass through the control.

I believe it was at the beginning of 1945, when Germany was nearing defeat, and train schedules had been disrupted both by the destruction of rail tracks and shortage of fuel, that parcels to inmates of Theresienstadt were limited to those sent from within a radius of one hundred kilometres. Through good Aryan friends and their relatives living in Czechoslovakia, my sister was able to continue sending parcels to our mother.

The criminal maladministration of the Jewish postal station in the camp changed only after employees and managers were finally fired and sentenced by a "ghetto court".

Receipt of a parcel could be confirmed by sending out a preprinted form card. "Dear ...., I confirm with thanks the receipt of your parcel of (date). Signature."

My mother was able to send us a few post-cards. Between the lines she wrote with the invisible ink and let us know what she needed most, either for herself or for barter, which was, of course, also considered illegal. This exchange system enabled her to get urgently required items which we were unable to send otherwise. She also managed to give us a little information about personal matters in the camp, yet not the full truth, because she did not want us to get worried.

One day we received a card on which the "invisible" had become visible. It must have been in the autumn of 1944, when the days were still warm enough to cause the water of the acid solution to evaporate from the bottle. Imagine our shock. And we did not realize then that deportees could be executed for the "crime" of smuggling uncensored information out of the camp. (Theresienstadt Camp Order B, paragraph 8, signed January 5th, 1943, the Camp Commandant, Dr. Seidl, SS-Hauptsturmführer.) [7]

My sister and I got together, and wrote a carefully worded post-card which went something like this: "Inge visited her girlfriend, who has to take stomach drops. This time, however, they did not agree with her at all, and we could see this right away from the colour of her face." After the liberation, my mother told me in Theresienstadt that when she received the card, she knew immediately what had gone wrong. She promptly stopped using the acid solution, most probably saving her life. None of us kept these interesting cards written with invisible ink, because we could never be sure whether — or when — a search by the Gestapo might take place.

When I had tried to visit my grandmother in Theresienstadt, and met inmates on my way to the Commandant, I had been surprised that men took off their caps and women bowed.

After the war, my mother explained to me that strict camp rules demanded such behaviour.

Here are the first five paragraphs of Chapter B, Special Part of Regulations, to throw some light on this matter:

1. The Ghetto-inmates have to greet every member of the camp detachment, of the SS-guard and government police by taking off their headgear. Women have to bow. Furthermore any person wearing uniform has to be greeted (as specified).

2. If talked to, (a Jew) has to stand at attention (in a direct translation:"...assume an erect posture").

3. If not told differently, a distance of one meter has to be kept.

4. The Ghetto-inmates are not permitted to speak to the persons mentioned under paragraph 1 without being asked to do so. Exceptions are made in cases of impending danger.

5. It is principally forbidden to drop in on the camp headquarters. Excepted are the Jew-elder and his deputy.

6. ... (etc.)

An old man, who was obviously confused, was said to have been killed merely because he did not pull his cap from his head fast enough.

My mother's work certificate shows that, after her arrival and stay at the Schleusse (sluice), she was assigned to quarters in the Bäckergasse 7 (Baker's Lane #7). She was then assigned to work at various auxiliary labour jobs — for instance, as part of a group of a hundred in the cleaning service, working at one time at the Hohe Elbe Hospital, or even shearing rabbits hair.

In April 1944, she was put to work in the Glimmerspalterei (mica splitting). The mineral crystals of mica have special insulating properties. These crystals can be split into extremely thin sheets which are used as insulators in electrical equipment. Germany needed a great deal of electrical equipment of many types for military purposes in the war she had started. The German military forces had given a contract for these mica sheets to Glimmerspalterei GmbH, who again employed slave labourers from the concentration camp through the Reich Security Headquarters (RSHA, SS and Gestapo.) While the inmates

Author's mother's work certificate at Theresienstadt

worked for practically nothing, the official employer, however, had to pay the RSHA a regular wage per employee. This method was used widely by the Nazis, as we shall see later, when I describe my deportation to a forced labour camp.

Working in mica splitting had its advantages and disadvantages. The work was very difficult and toilsome, and the dust was almost as dangerous as that from asbestos, which causes lung diseases. Bending over badly-lit tables for hours on end was very tiresome. However, since this work was of high strategic importance, and required well-trained personnel who could not be easily replaced, Jews working in this field had at least temporary protection from being deported to the gas-chambers in Eastern Europe. This circumstance may have saved my mother's life once more. She worked in the mica shop from September 7th, 1944, to the spring of 1945.

Her last job in the camp, though, was at the central laundry located on the other side of the Ohre (Eger) River. Czech gendarmes escorted the prisoners there and back. My mother was busy with many things. Sometimes she had to work the night shift, lasting from six o'clock in the evening until six o'clock the next morning. She especially liked the sorting part of the laundry work, because it was not only easier than anything she had to do in the camp before, but it was done in a warm building. Her supervisors and co-workers in all of her jobs liked her because she was always very accurate, clean and helpful. Her roommates told me this when I picked up my mother with my small, borrowed motor-cycle after Germany had finally been defeated.

2. — The Beautification Hoax

By the spring of 1944, the mass-slaughter of Jews by Nazi Einsatzgruppen (mobile killing units) and the SS — using machine guns, gas vans and gas chambers — had become more widely known to the Allies. Originally they had wondered whether or not this information was just atrocity propaganda, and some British politicians even maintained that this information could have been planted by the Jews themselves as a means of gaining access to Palestine. To discredit the leaks about the massacres, the Reichssicherheitshauptamt (RSHA, Reich Security Headquarters in charge of SS and Gestapo), in cooperation with the ministries for propaganda and for external affairs, planned an enormous cover-up and deception campaign.

The extermination camps in Eastern Europe were certainly not accessible to outsiders, such as neutral-country Red Cross officials, and the Nazis had not the slightest intention of opening these camps to any potential visitors. Concentration camps within the German Reich, like Buchenwald, Dachau, and Bergen-Belsen, could hardly be made presentable to neutral observers. But an idea was cooked-up to beautify Theresienstadt, and show it as a Paradise Ghetto to the Red Cross delegates of neutral countries.

Parts of Theresienstadt were reconstructed, including the Bäckergasse, where my mother had dwelled for a while. A former restaurant in the market square which had been turned into living quarters, was again remodelled to become a Kaffeehaus (café). A wooden music pavilion was erected close by. Trees were planted, flower-beds were designed and made, and some model barracks were built. Musical instruments were even brought in by the SS and orchestras were formed. In short: the works.

Prisoners said, "Once everything (the beautification) is done, we will all be transported to the East (to the extermination camps)".

There was "Kurmusik" (open-air concerts like at spas). My mother told me that a scene from "The Threepenny Opera" by Brecht-Weil was enacted and filmed outdoors, actually outside the concentration camp. She was recruited as one of the spectators. The whole area was, of course, surrounded by guards. Even so, the walk through the meadows to the show area, in the warming sun, was pure enjoyment compared to being caged in all the time.

So-called "Camp Currency" at Thersienstadt concentration camp.

At the end of the performance, ringing applause had to be given to satisfy the SS, who supervised everything. This sound was also recorded in the film. Quelle grande farce!

Another film was shot, showing people in party dresses dancing in the Kaffeehaus and outside. One could see Jews drinking coffee, laughing and appearing to be very relaxed, while listening to well-known melodies being played in the background. Very "Jewish-looking" people were selected as "actors." They were told to behave in a very leisurely manner. Mother was one of the chosen extras.

It was during fall of 1944 that I personally saw a short scene from this film under special circumstances. In the time following my escape, after the Allied Landing, I went to a movie theatre. Before the main feature came on screen, they always showed a newsreel. How surprised was I to see Theresienstadt! Jews sitting in the enjoyable atmosphere of a comfortable coffee house, eating cake and laughing — even muffled light music.

Scene changes: men and women, all well-dressed, are dancing, while a speaker can be heard saying:

"While Jews in Theresienstadt are enjoying coffee, cake and dancing..." — change of scene: battle, shooting, attacking, dirty soldiers, grenade explosions — "... our soldiers have to bear the brunt of a terrible war, misery and deprivation, in the defence of their fatherland." [10]

This was the way the Nazis were misleading the German people. The Germans who had heard rumours about the annihilation of Jews were given fake proof that not only were Jews not being hurt, they were actually living extremely comfortably at the expense of the average German, who was either in the war himself, or had close relatives exposed to death and injury.

The irony of it all was that the main actors and directors in this farce of a film, at first received gifts from the SS for their excellent performance, and then, only weeks later, were sent on "transports" to the gas chambers in the East.

3. — The Last Months in Theresienstadt

With the exception of short notes about the last days before Theresienstadt was taken over by the Soviets, mother did not keep a diary. Preparing such records was strictly forbidden by the SS authorities. In any event, for the average prisoner life was going on more or less the same way day by day. Also, because there were so many "bonkes" (rumours) circulating, one could never be sure what was true and what was not. One of these "bonkes" was that Hitler had cancer and had not much more time to live. Hearsay like this originated mostly from wishful thinking, and is common in all large restricted societies, especially in those where wishing and hoping is all that is left.

At the end of December 1944, all documents referring to deportation of Jews, such as statistical material in the hands of the Judenrat (Council of Jewish Elders), had to be handed over to the SS. These were at first stored, and then destroyed by the SS at the end of April 1945. The idea was to get rid of all incriminating evidence.

Here are my mother's short notes about the last days under the SS:

15 April 1945 — Danish citizens are transported home.

17/18 April 1945 — Rumours about a camp take-over by the Red Cross.

20/21 April 1945 — Arrival of new (prisoner) transports.

1 May 1945 — The prohibition on smoking is lifted. Everybody gets 3 cigarettes. Monsieur Paul Dunant of the Swiss Red Cross takes over the concentration camp.

5 May 1945 — SS move out of the Ghetto. SS-Oberstumführer Karl Rahm withdraws from his position in the evening hours.

6 May 1945 — The remaining Czech gendarmes leave. The SS-flag no longer flies from the mast above the city hall, the former commandant's headquarters: the Red Cross flag flies there now.

7 May 1945 — News about Germany's capitulation came through.

8 May 1945 — Machine-gun fire at the Schanze (entrenchment). Intensive shooting in the vicinity. [Theresienstadt was by then in the immediate combat zone. German military and SS were close by. Author]

Shooting very close at around 21:00 hrs. A Russian tank passes through Theresienstadt, although unnoticed by most Jews. Russians begin to march past our living quarters.

Had a lovely midnight stroll. [Something absolutely impossible to do during the SS regime in Theresienstadt. Author]

9 May 1945 — Walked through Theresienstadt. There was an air raid on Leitmeritz. More Russian troops come into Theresienstadt and throw cigarettes, tobacco, bread and sugar into the crowd. Prisoners of war come. [Germans? Author] *Risk of general epidemic. A lot of aircraft activity during the whole evening.*

10 May 1945 — We see again many Russian military driving by. They distribute cigarettes, etc. Bodenbacher was cleansed. [The Bodenbacher barracks and arsenal served the RSHA as archive for concentration camp documents which were evacuated from Berlin, because of the Allied air raids. Author]

Schorrn left [? Author] *Monsieur Dunant officially transfers the camp administration to a Russian officer, who imposes a strict quarantine on Theresienstadt because of spotted typhus and dysentery.*

[This quarantine was only partially relaxed by May 28th, 1945. Author]

12 May 1945 — Excursion to outside of town.

13 May 1945 — All transports (home) cancelled. Quarantine was announced to last at least fourteen days. Major Kusmin, Soviet Armed Forces, requests the first official roll call.

14 May 1945 — An American officer visits Theresienstadt and reports: no postal service in Germany. Most rail tracks and railway cars are destroyed.

15 May 1945 — American officer tells Gutfreund that all half-Jews get double food rations and American ration parcels (in the US Occupation Zone of Germany).

[This was not generally the case. Author]

It is said that more food will be made available for Theresienstadt. This started already with (the employees of) the (central) laundry.

16 May 1945 — Potato soup and sweetened barley! In the evening 1 pound of potatoes. Extra barley portions.

17 May 1945 — Bread.

25 May 1945 — Automobile from our hometown.

26 May 1945 — Mr. Weidlich went home.

I picked up my mother, and we left Theresienstadt on June 1st, 1945, three days before her fifty-third birthday.

Theresienstadt was closed as a camp in November 1945.

VI.— OCCUPIED FRANCE -

At the end of March 1944, I received an order to appear on a certain date and at a certain time at the labour exchange office in Plauen. On arrival, I recognized several other people of different ages, whom I knew casually. They were also of Jewish origin.

After a very cursory physical examination, we were all found fit for a so-far-unknown assignment. Somewhat later we were told that it had to do with short-term clearance work in bomb-damaged cities. We would have to be at the train-station on 4-4-44 (Who could forget such a date?) at a certain time early in the morning, with a suitcase containing what we would need for one to two weeks.

None of us were particularly suspicious, because many cities had really been heavily bombed by the Allies. Most Germans were in the armed forces, and many others could not be spared for such donkey work as clearance and salvage labour. On the other hand, the Nazis would never hesitate to round us up anyway, if they wanted to. But we did not have the feeling like Volljuden (Full Jews), expecting to be deported to concentration camps. Admittedly, we were naive.

As we arrived at the train station that day, we were surprised to see Gestapo men waiting for us. We were ordered to get aboard a regularly scheduled train, but in a special car which had been reserved by the Gestapo. The compartment doors were then locked and two Gestapo officials escorted us to Dresden. Later, we realized that other compartments had also been reserved, because other detainee groups boarded on our way to Dresden.

When we arrived, there was already quite a crowd in a separated part of the huge station hall. All exits were closely guarded. I guess there were fifteen hundred to two thousand people. Almost everybody seemed to be talking, and the racket was tremendous. In the afternoon, the noise suddenly died down when shouts of command could be heard and armed personnel marched up. There were SS troops and, with them, Italian soldiers in their olive-grey uniforms. We were divided into groups, and, fortunately, all the men from Plauen managed to stay together when we were led in batches onto the platform. Before we were assigned to specific train carriages, we were told by the SS that our escorts had been given orders to shoot without warning if somebody tried to leave the train. This was quite a different tone from what we had heard about the harmless clearance work to be done.

The train left in the evening for an unknown destination. We tried to find out where we were going, but during the night it was impossible to read station signs because of the blackout, and during the day we saw only unfamiliar names. So the great guessing game began. Obviously, we were not on main lines. For many reasons, we had very long stops. Our train surely was not a scheduled one; a great part of both railway lines and installations had been destroyed, and military transports were given preference.

At one point, someone said we had to be in the Rhineland. That made sense to us, because places along the Rhine, like Cologne and the Ruhr region, had been targets for many Allied bombing raids. Again, we had guessed wrong.

After many hours we saw French signs and, shortly after, all sorts of rumours spread through the train. I remember one person saying that someone had heard the name, "Biarritz," from the escorts.

After about two days and repeated long stops, we reached Paris. Up to that moment we had not been allowed to leave the train, not even to get some drinking water. Then there were commands, lining up and separation into groups. Eventually,

Caserne Mortier, Paris. Gate and Barracks building

busses brought us from the Gare de l'Est to some barracks, called Caserne Mortier [11], in the northeast of the city, not far from the Metro station, Porte des Lilas. We found that French Jews were already imprisoned there.

Later, or maybe it was the next day, we had to rush to a roll-call in the barrack-yard, where the commander — as we learned later, SS-Obersturmführer Müller — with a submachine gun hanging from his shoulder, gave us "valuable" information (as if we had not heard this kind of song before). Because of our Jewish descent, we were not worthy to be part of the German people's community. At this point, we also learned that on the "transport" with us were criminals, "political unreliables", homosexuals and Gypsies. The Gypsies fell into the same category as we did, because their disgrace was also hereditary. It was simply "in their blood", Müller said. In contrast to us, the criminals, political detainees and homosexuals could become useful German citizens again, so it was shouted at us across the barrack-square. Those of us with Jewish and Gypsy blood, however, were, by Nazi definition, sub-human, both then and forever more.

Just to make sure he was properly understood, Müller mentioned that, in St.Cloud, a district of Paris, was a special SS "correction" centre, which could deal with all kinds of problems.

After the roll-call, we were each given a number, and then photos were taken. Back in the barrack-yard, we were divided into groups of a hundred men and finally sent to the sleeping halls. There was no longer any doubt about our real status — we had become prisoners of the SS

1. — Valognes — [12]

Three hundred of us left the next day for Valognes, district La Manche, roughly twenty kilometres south-southeast of Cherbourg, Normandy, on the Cotentin peninsula. This "transport" was escorted by armed German OT-men (Organization Todt, a para-military organization) and armed Italian soldiers.

In Valognes was an old Pensionnat de Jeunes Filles [13][14], which consisted of three main buildings, surrounding a courtyard in horseshoe fashion. It has survived bombings and battles and still exists. From one of the main streets in town, one entered through a gate into a front court and then the centre building. This was occupied by the administration offices, quarters for the commandant and the guards, the kitchen, storage area and a first-aid room. In the two remaining wing-buildings were the sleeping quarters of the prisoners. Each of the rooms on the ground floor was directly accessible from the courtyard. All upper-floor rooms could be reached from the ground by either of the two staircases which led to a gallery in front of these rooms, each of which held bunkbeds for twenty to twenty-five men. There was just one threadbare blanket and one straw mattress per prisoner, with the straw being a fantastic breeding milieu for many species of vermin. The rooms were terribly drafty and also cold because they were not heated when we were there.

The washing facility was a trough-like basin located outside of only one building on the ground floor and gave nothing but cold water.

Equally limited were the latrines located at the open end of the horseshoe construction. The whole complex was surrounded by barbed wire fencing, and armed guards were always posted at the exit.

All but one of the Plauen gang manoeuvred to stay together in the same room. Then we found out that we had two criminals among us, and managed to exchange one of them for a missing fellow from Plauen, who, by accident, had wound up in another room. The second "crimie" tried to betray us. He had been planted by the Commandant as an informer, which pretty soon became unmistakably clear to us. Once we had solid proof of his activity, we confronted him with the evidence and beat the daylights out of him. Incidentally, it was my role to hit him over

Valognes. Now Ecole Ste-Marie, used in 1944 as a forced labour camp

the head with the tin bowl in which I received my portion of the "bunker soup". From that moment on, the man did not dare to say one more word to the camp authorities. He knew that, if he divulged anything we had discussed, he would meet with a sudden accident and have no one in the room to defend him. We did not try to get him out of our room, because the camp commandant, Obertruppführer Leutner, would have smelled a rat, and would have distributed our gang over several rooms. This one criminal therefore became guarantor of our security — and our staying together.

Unknown to Leutner and his men, we developed ways of finding out relatively quickly the background of each prisoner. Those of Jewish origin or married to Jews, usually knew enough Yiddish to signal their identity. Moreover, these inmates came from Western Germany, which in those days meant Rhineland, Badenia, etc., or from Saxony such as our group.

In our camp, all Gypsies and Gypsy-descendants from mixed marriages came from East Prussia. Even though some were sixty to sixty-five years old, they had all been sterilized by Nazi butcher-doctors. None of them had led the proverbial nomadic Gipsy life, but had been settled with their families in villages and towns for generations. Most of them were farmers.

In the beginning, when they did not enjoy a preferred position, the criminals were very ill-at-ease, and we could sense it. They did not trust any of their own kind, let alone anyone else.

Most of the homosexuals could be readily identified, as they did not make any attempt to hide their easily recognizable behaviour.

Rumour had it that even Obertruppführer (Otf.) Leutner had come into conflict with the law. However, because he fought after World War I in a right-wing organization, one of the infamous Freikorps, in the Baltic Provinces, and had been decorated with the Baltic Cross which he wore on his uniform at all times, he had become useful in the eyes of the Nazis.

After the Italian escort soldiers had left, we were guarded by armed OT-men. The supreme authority, however, was the SS.

Otf. Leutner received his orders from the SS-headquarters in Paris, who in turn got their orders from the Reich Security Headquarters (RSHA) in Berlin. Leutner was a skinny, drivelling man, who hid his insecurity behind his uniform, his medal, his gigantic Mauser pistol, and his subordinates, who wore OT-uniforms but had swastika armbands, normally not part of the OT dress code.

We had two days to get settled in the camp, during which time we also received camp garb made from ticking.

What had been concealed behind the facade of "clearance work" or "alternative service" was, for the inmates of our particular camp, work on the Atlantic Wall, which was a German defence system in the occupied countries along the Atlantic coast. The Atlantic Wall was constructed by the Germans in an attempt to prevent Allied troops from landing. Under construction within this defence system were certain rocket launching areas, where launching ramps, bunkers, access roads, etc., were to be built. Needless to say, these tactical construction sites were constantly exposed to Allied bombing raids. Details about this will follow.

As we learned later, prisoners like us in other slave labour camps in France were also given different tasks, such as disarming blind bombs at military airports, detecting landmines (placed in strategic regions by resistance fighters), and working in other dangerous places, e.g. underwater caissons of harbours.

It is not difficult to see why we were chosen for this special privilege of work for an insane Führer/Reich combination. Germans were considered too valuable to be killed or wounded at such jobs; our kind of people was considered expendable.

Apart from a few exceptional days, our food was poor and consisted mainly of soup made from water with cabbage, potatoes or turnips; at times these soups were even hardly salted. We called that stuff "bunker soup". Most times, the moist and mouldy bread we received could not be considered fit for human consumption. Spoiled food, from what the military and the SS left over or rejected, was sent to our camp. Besides, we got very small rations of margarine and jam. Morning and evening, each room received a pot of ersatz coffee (substitute coffee). Basically, we were fed just enough to keep us at a basic work strength.

Very occasionally, we succeeded in bribing the kitchen help for paltry little pieces of meat, which were then distributed among the roommates in a fair way. However, such methods of food procurement were extremely risky. If someone was caught bribing kitchen personnel, he was immediately sent to the SS penal-camp in Tourlaville. Now and then one of us was lucky enough to get a little precious food from French civilian workers, which was always greatly appreciated.

With one of the OT-men screaming in the courtyard at 5:00 a.m., we woke up to reality. Each one of us wrapped himself tightly in his sole blanket when we left at 6:00 or 6:30 a.m., since it was the only protection against the usually very cold wind, when we were driven in the open trucks to the construction sites. Especially when it was grey and dark, these were really sad, ghastly loads being carried through the otherwise beautiful countryside of Normandy.

Around 12:00 noon, a truck brought our bunker soup.

In the beginning we did not know the final purpose of these construction sites. Later, when we had made contact with Dutch people in other forced labour units, we learned that we were building bunkers and concrete platforms for rocket launching ramps.

The V-rockets were actually the first long-range missiles to be built, and were then in their final stage of development. "V" stood for Vengeance (German: Vergeltung), and there were two types of V-missiles. The V-1 came first and was called "buzz-bomb" by the Allies, because of the kind of noise the motor made. It could also be called a drone, because it was practically a small pilotless plane. The V-2 was a supersonic missile. Fortunately, the Germans had only a very limited production capacity for these rockets. Even now I do not know which kind of missile the Germans had planned to launch from the sites we were working on, because the emplacement was never completed. But more about this later.

Most of the time our job consisted of carrying steel-reinforced concrete beams and heavy bags of cement. Moving the beams had to be done in the most primitive way. Eight men, in pairs of four, had to push four wooden poles under the ferro-concrete beam and then get a good grip on the poles. At the guard's command we had to lift the six-meter long thing. Once I was viciously beaten by a guard, just because he wanted me to take a different grasp on such a pole. The work was not only very hard but also dangerous, because of the bombardments of the construction site by Allied aircraft. Camp posts such as kitchen help or craftsmen were very desirable because, as a rule, they were neither strenuous nor perilous. On the other hand, cleaning service in the camp was not much in demand, because this crew, among other tasks, had to empty the frequently overflowing latrines, not designed for three hundred-plus people.

It was back-breaking labour out at the construction sites, particularly during the first weeks, because we were not used to such manual work. [15]

Aside from the fact that there was only limited access to washing facilities, we were so exhausted in those early weeks when we came back each evening between 6:00 and 6:30 p.m. that, after roll-call, we just fell on our straw mattresses, ate from our bowls there, and fell asleep. No attempt was made at washing, be it body or clothes, nor did anyone think about mending holes in socks or sewing damaged clothing.

We were allowed to write one letter per week, so long as no mention was made of locations, names, living or working conditions. These letters had to be handed to the administration office in an open envelope, so that they could be censored later by the SS, presumably at a postal centre in Paris. A certain mail code-number had to be given as sender, so that any incoming mail would also be channelled through this SS-office. Unless one had made arrangements with friends concerning the use of a cipher, nobody back in Germany could find out where we were.

As already mentioned, the camp was infested with vermin. After our room leader complained repeatedly and very seriously about this problem, Otf. Leutner finally gave in and ordered the purchase of an insecticide. However, either this product had already exceeded its shelf-life, or the chemical per se was ineffective; whatever the reason, the parasites were definitely not affected by it. Even repeated applications proved to be useless.

We came to believe that the product actually increased the fleas' joy for procreation and biting.

In our room were two brothers, Hans and Walter U. Walter, who was a physician, became a victim of this vermin infestation. Because the best posts in the camp were nearly always given to criminals, the man in charge of first aid was not a doctor, but a totally unqualified person, and a mean jerk at that. Criminals could get from him all the medication they needed or wanted. People with Gypsy or Jewish backgrounds were constantly refused help. There was, of course, hostility and tension between the two groups of prisoners, criminals and racially "undesirables". Although the criminals really had nothing to be proud of, they nonetheless prided themselves on having a "clean" ancestry and formed a sort of camp-Mafia. Many times, these characters showed more vicious Jew-hatred than our guards, and this is probably why some of them were chosen to become guards in the months ahead.

Dr. Walter U. was bitten by fleas, more badly than anybody else in the whole camp. What was worse, the bites got infected and his legs became so swollen that eventually he could hardly stand up. When he went to see the first-aid person and requested a disinfectant and bandages, the guy laughed and said that nobody needs medical attention because of flea bites. Then Walter U. had to report sick because he was unable to work. The first-aider reported this to the camp commandant, just loving the opportunity to trip up the person he felt was his rival. In a way, Walter may have unintentionally appeared as a rival, because camp inmates went to see him, rather than the first-aider, when they had any real medical problems. Leutner decided that Dr. U.

was not unfit for work, but just too lazy.

Walter was brought under guard to the SS-camp in Tourlaville for punishment. He was tortured in a most bestial way. Apart from beating prisoners mercilessly, one of the methods the SS applied was to let them crawl on their unprotected underarms several times over a fifty meter gravel track. When Walter was brought back, his clothes were torn, he was dirty and his whole body was bleeding and shaking.

From the gate, he barely made it into our room and there he collapsed. While he was still unconscious, Otf. Leutner screamed from the yard for Walter to come down. We started to hastily clean his face with water and, when Walter began to come to, Hans helped his brother down the stairs, supporting him so that he could stand in front of Leutner and the two SS-men who had brought him back from Tourlaville. One of the SS-men screamed at Walter: "What did you want to say when you came back here?" In a hardly audible voice Walter answered: "I would like so much to work right now." This is what they had pounded into his head at Tourlaville. And just to make life more miserable for him, two prisoners had to bring a saw-horse with a big piece of tree trunk on it, which Walter had to saw. Being completely exhausted, Walter collapsed again. Hans helped him up, took a firm grip on the other side of the bow saw, and started to work on the wood. Walter just hung on, being unable to muster any strength for the job, and was simply pulled back and pushed forth by Hans.

Before Walter was permitted to go back to our room, he was explicitly told that at no time was he allowed to give medical advice to camp inmates.

At almost every roll-call, we were threatened with Tourlaville.

Things reached a peak shortly before the Allied Landing in France. Some of the guards had already been replaced by criminal inmates, who must have received cash-pay each time before they were allowed to have leave from the camp for a few hours. On one occasion, they were totally drunk when they returned and, when one of them started to hit one of our roommates, we all jumped on him, pulled him into the room, locked the door from the inside and beat the living daylights out of him. The man was so startled that we had no problem taking his pistol away from him. Otf. Leutner yelled in front of the door and threatened to shoot, but we remained firm in our demand that armed prisoners should no longer be allowed to drink alcohol.

This extremely volatile situation was dangerous for us; it is so easy to ignite rage under desperate conditions. Quite possibly, the reason Leutner beat a retreat was because he could have been punished himself for letting prisoners have access to alcohol. Leutner saved face with a compromise: we had to stand for one hour in the cold yard, and he then promised that he would not tolerate drunkenness of guards or guard replacements.

Although the homosexuals in our camp did not openly show affection for one another, they made no attempt to hide their inclinations either. Kurt W. preferred to be called Rosa, spoke with a strange and unnaturally high voice, moved about with feminine motions, and was happy that he had been given a job inside the camp.

One night I went to the latrine, even though we were not allowed to leave the rooms during these night hours. The moon was shining and it seemed everybody was fast asleep. When I returned and was walking up the stairs, somebody grabbed me from behind. With a sudden move I turned around, and hit the prowler so hard with the back of my fist, that he fell down the stairs. It was Rosa W. He started whining and implored me not to make any noise or to report him to the camp authorities. In a way feeling sorry for the guy, I agreed to keep quiet if he would promise not to make any more advances. Somewhat hesitatingly, he asked if I would allow him to mend my socks and wash my clothes. Being worn out from each day's work, like everybody else, I could certainly do without these chores, so I agreed.

Once during a roll-call, Otf. Leutner announced that SS-officers would inspect the camp in a week or two, and ordered us to produce a variety show for their amusement. A small stage had to be erected, and five or six SS-officers came. They sat on folding-chairs in front of the stage. As far as the exact numbers and details of the show are concerned, my memory lets me down. One act, however, I remember well: Rosa W. in a pink, formal lady's dress, with a bouquet of flowers in his (her?) arms and singing with his raspy female-imitation voice: "... buy beautiful roses you handsome men ..." His face was made up with a heavy layer of powder over his shaved face, yet not covering fully the dark hair of the beard underneath. The SS-officers roared with laughter, and most of us felt very embarrassed about the spectacle which had been presented to our tormentors.

Actually, this was the only time we saw the SS laugh in our presence.

2. — Marching through Valognes

On Sundays we did not have to work on the construction sites, as nobody else was there, and part of the guard unit used to be on leave in town. For us prisoners, it was the big clean-up day of the week, reserved for cleaning the camp, the rooms, our clothing and ourselves. In the afternoon, Otf. Leutner always ordered a roll-call. He cursed the synagogues and churches as source of all evil, and threatened us every time with transfer to Tourlaville and getting shot.

Afterwards, we had to march in formation through Valognes, with him prancingly leading the way. The question, why marching through the streets with three hundred constantly-guarded prisoners obviously lifted his self-esteem, always puzzled me. But somehow it must have given him an ego boost. We had to learn two marching songs for the outings, and were ordered to sing them at the top of our voices. Part of the text of one was (in translation): "There, where the clouds pass at the edge of the forest, lies the new era." The last four words had to be repeated as a refrain, and some of us replaced these with singing instead "lies the Fourth Reich", meaning: it's the end of the "Third Reich."

Of course, the new words were drowned out by the others, but it was nonetheless one of several such psychological safety-valves — inexplicable acts — we used to vent our rage and to reduce some of our frustrations.

Although, otherwise, we marched like a bunch of zombies through Valognes, we kept our eyes open. What we sensed and saw, gave us some hope for the long expected Allied invasion, even though we did not expect this to happen right in the backyards of Valognes.

There were V-shaped chalk signs, "V" for Allied victory. We passed posters saying "La France a perdu une battaille, mais la France n'a pas perdu la guerre!" (France lost a battle, but France has not lost the war!)

Italy had broken away from her alliance with Germany in September 1943, and the Anglo-American forces had landed at Nettuno on January 22nd, 1944. We noticed placards, put up by the resistance, showing the advance of Allied armies through boot-shaped Italy. It always took the Germans a while to paint over or remove such signs of rebellion against the occupation forces.

Word also got through to us that Hungary seemed willing to end their participation in the war, and the Soviets were advancing rapidly through Eastern Europe.

I may have been able to describe some, but certainly not all the conditions in our camp. Obviously, to a degree, our plight had an effect on each of us, and this was certainly not unique to the Valognes Camp. Some men became inconsiderate, even reckless, and grew brutal, while others became helpful and caring beyond their usual kindness. Yet again, others showed a friendly face but informed against their fellow prisoners. It seemed, both the best and the worst in people surfaced under these trying circumstances. One unfortunate chap lost his nerves completely. Whenever there was an air-raid, he stormed into the nearest room, crept into a corner, and held his arms over his head, even though the building structure would not have offered the slightest protection. We teasingly called him "Bombs-Willie."

At the end of May, rumours began circulating that plans had been made to begin with the sterilization of Jewish "Mischlinge (literally: half-casts) of the first degree." In the Nazi jargon these were persons of Jewish descent with two Jewish grandparents. This was to be done in the same way the Nazis had already sterilized the Gypsies. To what extent the preparations for this project had finally progressed, we will probably never know.

Years later we learned that this matter had already been discussed at the beginning of the forties. It was then brought up again as a serious issue at the infamous Wannsee Conference on January 20th, 1942, and later on March 6th of the same year with Adolf Eichman as chairman of that conference on the "final solution." In the end it was agreed on the high levels of the Nazi hierarchy that "Mischlinge" would have to be definitely eliminated from the German People's Community in one way or another.

The harshest of slave labour under Allied air attacks was one of these methods.

In our case most likely, the Allied invasion thwarted further developments of the intended sterilization.

I became seriously ill with a stomach problem, and was sent for treatment to a German Army hospital. They had orders to treat me no longer than a week, even if there was no improvement. The surgeon-major, a mean type of person, swore at me when I arrived, but, fortunately, left on home leave the next day. His deputy was kindness personified and made me feel like I was in heaven-on-earth.

Not only did I get intensive care for my illness, but they gave me all the good food they could possibly make available to bring my strength back. I was more pampered than I had ever been since childhood. A Catholic priest, who served in the army as hospital orderly, also did all he could trying to soothe my spiritual as well as physical wounds, all totally without hidden motives. He was just a really good human being.

My stomach problems had dramatically improved by the time one of our guards picked me up. I had in my pocket a few thousand francs and several packages of saccharin tablets; the latter were valuable bartering commodities and all was a gift from the doctor and the priest.

In retrospect, this short interlude was like a dream, fleeting and unreal.

Going back to the camp and the hard labour at the construction site was like jumping from heaven to hell — the cold, dirty and vermin-infested rooms, the putrid smell from the latrines, the constantly gnawing hunger, the mockery and abuse during roll-calls; the exposure again to unaccustomed heavy labour, as well as the bombardments at the work place . . . all this was a complex dantesque trauma, mental as well as physical. Only the company of good fellow-inmates and the will to survive made these days bearable.

3. — At the Atlantic Wall

If one listened to the Nazi propaganda, the Atlantic Wall seemed to be a continuous, impenetrable defence line with one fortification next to another. But this was not quite so. At strategic points the Germans had build pill-boxes or other tactical strongholds, but when Field marshal Rommel inspected the Atlantic Wall on May 11th, 1944, he was not satisfied and ordered more work to be done. Even so, nothing much changed afterwards. A basic weakness of this system was that all major defence weapons aimed toward the sea. If attacked from behind, as would actually happen, they offered no protection at all.

We worked at the planned missile launching sites carrying steel-concrete elements, pouring cement, etc., merely to rebuild what had been destroyed in frequent raids by Allied bombers.

Although all structures were camouflaged by either paint, trees, branches or coloured nets, they must have been easily detectable by infrared photography used by the Anglo-American reconnaissance pilots.

The Allies did all they could to knock out any launching sites for the new aerial weapons. They wanted to eliminate any counter attacks on D-Day (day of the Allied Invasion of Europe and the landing of Allied armed forces in Normandy.) Undisturbed by the German Luftwaffe — the Allies had absolute air superiority — "our daily reconnaissance plane", as we called the low-flying Mosquito planes, took photographs of the entire area. Post-war documentation has shown, over one million maps were produced from such photos in preparation for the invasion assault, and were distributed to the attack forces. These photos were also used as confirmation of reports received from the Armée Secrète. About a year before the invasion, Colonel Remy of the Résistance had succeeded in getting a map, showing exact specifications of all German positions in precisely the region planned for the invasion.

It appears that the Allies did not want to waste their bombs. They carefully watched the progress that was made in building the launching sites, waited until the installations were almost finished, then, and only then, did they send their medium bombers to destroy them with precision bombing. [16]

Unfortunately for us, these bombers had such a short approach route that we did not get a well-timed warning of an impending raid. By the time the German sirens in Cherbourg sounded the air-raid warning, the bombers were already over our construction site. These bomber attacks were not only horrifying because of their powerful physical effect, but almost equally so from the psychological point of view. The roaring of the approaching bombers, the howling when they came down for a low-altitude strike, the explosions, and the fact that we had no air-raid shelter or other means of protection, gave us a feeling of total helplessness. Again, we were in the situation of sitting ducks, lined up in front of a firing squad.

Quite a few prisoners were killed this way, among them my good friend, Gerhard L., with whom I had once gathered mushrooms in the German woods.

Hans U., brother of Walter the physician, was not a man to get upset or scared easily. He was experienced, had a cool head and took everything in his stride. I vividly remember my surprise during one of these air-raids. When the bombers attacked, Hans ran blindly, as if he could escape the aircraft by fleeing on foot. Screaming unintelligibly, he held his blanket over his head like a horizontal sail and eventually fell into the barbed-wire enclosure. Fortunately, he was neither killed nor wounded by the bomb splinters. This was a typical panic reaction under such circumstances, but not what one would expect from Hans, and, in fact, it never happened again, as far as I know.

At the beginning of 1944, the Chief Representative for Allocation of Labour (Generalbeauftragter für den Arbeitseinsatz) decided to take half-a-million people out of the Netherlands for labour tasks. Many were deported to France to work in forced labour units, some to construction sites as we were on.

Once these labourers from German-occupied countries knew who was who in our crew and they had overcome their initial suspicions, they taught us how to sabotage by adding higher portions of sand into the cement mix than specified, or by using salt to make the concrete brittle.

The Dutch had connections to a secret transmitting station in the Cherbourg area and received warnings about imminent air attacks on the construction sites. Once they knew who could be trusted, they gave us this information. We in turn found ways of hinting to the guards that there was probably danger on a certain day at a certain time. The guards, who were just as unprotected as we were when bombs started falling, did not ask any questions, but were glad to take us outside the built-up areas into the woods. From then on, no more lives were lost, and no more of our people were wounded or killed.

Although officially we were not permitted to talk with anybody, it was impossible for the guards to enforce this rule at the construction site. Of necessity, we had to have contact with those who were supervising our work, and with those who had been recruited from several occupied countries, had lighter work than we did, but were tied into the missile site construction program just the same. Incidentally, as it turned out, these workers became an invaluable and willing source of information for Allied intelligence.

Being otherwise cut off from the outside world, we learned many things through our Dutch friends. They lived in mass quarters and were driven to and from the construction sites in trucks, but were free to spend their spare time as they pleased. They could walk around Cherbourg, visit restaurants or taverns, and talk with whomever they pleased.

From them, we heard about the activities of the French underground army (Armée Secrète) which, since about the time we had arrived in Valognes, were called "Forces Françaises de l'Intérieur (FFI)". Being guided by their headquarters in London, the FFI-résistance prepared and carried out sabotage acts as groundwork for the forthcoming invasion and the Allied battles in France. We were also told that dock workers from Cherbourg, who had fled into the hinterland, were asked to stand by for the expected invasion and to help then unloading Allied ships. Furthermore, they mentioned to us the coast was mined, wired and spiked. Some metal stakes were not readily visible, because they were submerged in the coastal waters. Obstacles such as mined stakes were called "Czech hedgehogs."

On our way to the construction sites, we wondered what the slanting poles in the flat fields were for. Later we learned that they were called "Rommel Asparagus", intended to damage or destroy landing aircraft and gliders in case of an invasion, and to wound or kill landing troops on impact. There were mines attached to the tops of some of these poles. Frenchmen between the ages of eighteen and sixty had to work one day a week for the Germans, and some of them had to set up these Rommel Asparagus poles.

Our Dutch friends warned us to be on our guard, because

for every loyal and brave man in the Résistance there was at least one French collaborator, who would gladly inform the SS and Gestapo about any conspiratorial act.

As time went on, we had to build the bunker walls and ramps thinner and thinner. The last structures were actually nothing more than shelters, made from hollow concrete blocks. Damage to the railway system, caused partly by bombing and partly by sabotage, led to considerable delays in the delivery of construction materials. The shortage of cement became more and more acute, especially after a cement plant in Cherbourg had to be shut down due to shortage of coal. As a result of the repeated bombing and shortage of construction material, the missile launching ramps, at least in our area, were never finished. [16]

4. — Will there be an Invasion?

My brother-in-law-to-be, Corri, who had been deported from Holland to Germany with a forced labour unit, had given me two addresses in the Netherlands. They were contact addresses of underground movements. One of them brought Jewish and other refugees through occupied Belgium and France to neutral Spain; the other helped fugitives from the Nazis by putting them on board small Allied seaplanes, which picked up people from boats on the Zuiderzee. These are very interesting stories in themselves, and there is published literature about them.

Corri said that if I ever reached Holland, I should try to see these men at the addresses given to me; they were reliable. [17]

I had written these secret addresses in the smallest possible handwriting and always hid them well on my body, day and night. In the claws of the Gestapo, at the beginning of 1945, I was fortunate to have been able to put these notes into my mouth and chew and swallow them.

One of the Dutch men at our construction site seemed to me to be especially friendly and helpful. Using concrete walls as screens to hide, we discussed and planned how to get me out of the labour camp. He was due for home leave in the middle of June. From his contact in Cherbourg he could get forged travel and leave documents for me, but not valid identification papers. Yet, I was willing to take the risk.

In exchange for a pair of new boots, stolen from the camp storage room, part of my saccharin supply and one thousand francs, I got the two leave permits. We worked hard on the correct Dutch pronunciation of a few basic words and phrases. The best chance for escape would have been during an air-raid, when we would be evacuated by the guards from the restricted work area. Finally, everything was prepared for a go for the middle of June. But then ...

The Allies were bombing France constantly. Were these air-raids in our area only diversionary tactics to prepare for an invasion somewhere else? In these days we lived in an atmosphere of anticipation and general uncertainty, but nonetheless felt that something was going to happen in the near future. There was definitely something in the wind.

By planting misinformation, the Allies had managed to convince the German Military High Command that there would be a landing operation in the Pas-de-Calais region, which was where the distance across the English Channel was the shortest. Field marshal Rommel, however, was convinced that the Allies would strike against the Brittany and Cotentin peninsulas. Originally Hitler shared Rommel's views, but then changed his mind. Some literature sources give details about all the different views of the Nazi and German military hierarchies during this pre-invasion period.

One day my Dutch friend told me that the BBC would broadcast the first part of a poem by the French poet, Paul Verlaine, to notify the French Resistance to prepare for the invasion. The second part of this poem would then indicate that the invasion was to take place within forty-eight hours.

On June 2nd — it must have been a Friday — I saw my friend at the construction site, waiting impatiently for the chance to speak to me. With great excitement, he informed me that the night before, the BBC had broadcast from "Chanson d'Automne" . . . "Les sanglots longs des violons de l'automne." When I told my Plauen buddies about it, they became as filled with suspense as I was. We were so nervous that, from then on, we were actually unable to do things with "un ésprit clair."

"Tight lips" was the motto and not a word was mentioned to anybody outside our group. What we did not hear, however, was that, on the night of June 5th, 1944, the BBC transmitted the second line: ". . . bercent mon coeur d'une langueur monotone". That night the invasion began, and we never went back to any of the construction sites.

To my greatest regret, I never saw my Dutch friend again.

5. — The Invasion

As far as the weather was concerned, the month of May had been quite pleasant. By contrast, the first days of June were grey, cool, rainy and very windy. Nonetheless, Otf. Leutner had, as usual, demanded a march through Valognes on Sunday, June 4th, 1944. Once again, we had sung our protest refrain "... there lies the new era, THE FOURTH REICH", drowned out by the many voices who sang the correct version. Cold and wet, we returned to the camp. Monday was business as usual, i.e., getting up early in the morning, working at the construction site, returning late, eating bunker soup and drinking weak ersatz-coffee.

My set of spare clothes was clean and my socks mended, thanks to Rosa W. So I could hit the (straw) sack early, in order to rest and recover my energies.

By this time in the evening, the rain had stopped.

If I remember correctly, it was shortly after midnight when we were wakened by an air-raid alarm. At the same time we heard the droning of aircraft, typical of bombers flying in formation. They came right over Valognes, one wave after another. That made us immediately jump out of our bunk beds, dress and run into the roll-call yard. For reasons which never became known to us, and to our greatest surprise, there was no guard at the gate and the gate itself was actually open. We did not hesitate long, but stormed out of the camp, through the streets and into the fields, looking for cover.

The winds were still gusty, and the clouds low. The droning went on. Thousands of bombers must have flown over Valognes that night. [18] They set bright flares, many of them large parachute flares, looking like luminous Christmas trees and staying in the air for a very long time. Most of them were dropped over the Montebourg area, approximately eight kilometres from Valognes, in the direction of Ste. Mère-Eglise.

As I was lying in a good position in the field, surrounded by little mounds of soil, I thought that the illumination was so intense that one would be able to read a newspaper.

None of our clique had the vaguest notion what these flares were for. Maybe the lead planes had marked the area for bombing. We knew only one thing almost for sure, namely that the invasion had begun. Strangely enough, we did not hear explosions. It turned out, that the flares had been set to mark the dropping zones for airborne landings.

I heard constant anti-aircraft fire, and could see some AA tracer bullets, but it seemed to me that there were only isolated German flak batteries in the Valognes region.

Any attempt to understand our emotions during these hours would be futile. We could feel the enormity of the destructive forces coming, and imagine the lives that would be lost and the blood that would be spilled. Yet these sentiments were mixed with a joyous anticipation of an ending of the horrible Nazi regime in the not too distant future. We watched with astonishment "le grand spectacle" of fireworks of a hitherto unseen magnitude. One felt like bursting out laughing with joy, but at the same time felt very afraid for what might evolve before one could see the end, sit down and sigh in complete relief. It was total bewilderment.

I am in doubt about the exact time, but it was probably around 3:00 a.m. when artillery shells of all calibres started howling through the night. They came from ship batteries. The "biggies", the heavy shells which we called "schwere Koffer" (heavy suitcases), made a peculiar vacillating sound, a hooting with slightly changing sound frequency, as they moved toward their targets. Large and medium planes bombed the areas behind the beaches. Fighter-bombers strafed the roads and German positions. It was a gigantic inferno. Volley after volley came from the navy cannons, illuminating the horizon like summer lightening.

At dawn, we gathered in the field and discussed what to do. The situation was anything but clear. When we had marched through Valognes two days earlier, we had seen men from Waffen-SS divisions, but also units of regular German military.

Since we had no way of knowing how to assess the present state of affairs, we reluctantly decided to go back to the camp first and reconnoitre how things really stood, instead of coming to a rash conclusion about our next move.

An escape is reasonable only if one is able to make a decision based on the assessment of a situation, using all available facts. At this point we knew pitifully little, and, therefore, were not able to appraise our chances. Almost all of the prisoners who escaped that night eventually returned to the camp, most probably having reasoned things out in much the same way our Plauen gang had done.

Daylight came, but no command to get on a truck for the ride to a construction site. There were no trucks. Prisoners were standing in groups in the yard debating the events as far as we had observed them. Nobody shouted an order to stand in formation for a roll-call. There was a strange disarray, with armed guards standing around not knowing what to do.

When Otf. Leutner finally came down from his room, he looked not only pale, but almost white. His uniform was open at the collar and his speech was incoherent. He alternately screamed and talked normally. Obviously his nerves were completely shot.

The next thing I remember was a banging on the gate, when an SS-man on a motor-cycle asked to speak to Otf. Leutner. We found out later that Leutner had to transfer all but one of the official OT-guards to fighting units, and replace them with "reliable" people from the camp. Leutner had no scruples about selecting criminals, as he had already done before. There was this one remaining OT-man, who became his deputy. Consequently, all but one of the armed guards were looking to us and the Gypsies for revenge. Now they could prove their reliability to Leutner, and their worthiness for the Nazi regime, simply by ill-treating people with Jewish blood in their veins.

At noon we got our bunker soup. Around 2:00 p.m., the air-raid alarm sounded. Even though the buildings had no shelters, this time we were not permitted to leave the camp. This raid was the first bombardment of Valognes and it hit the Quartier d'Alleaume where we had been the previous night. Otf. Leutner did not show his face. Bombs-Willie almost jumped out of his skin. Fortunately, our camp was not hit then.

It was relatively quiet during the night. On Wednesday, June 7th, there was another bombardment of Valognes. Again, we were not allowed to leave the camp. The bombs were dropped near the train station and hit a convent, the Couvent du Bon Sauveur. This bombing created such a panic among the prisoners that it was impossible to control them, and, since the guards were just as scared as we were, they did not offer much resistance when some of the prisoners broke out of the camp.

After the raid, a few of them did not come back, but, unfortunately, most of them were caught shortly afterwards by SS or Geheime Feldpolizei (Secret Military Police.) We never learned what happened to them.

A German encyclopaedia from the Nazi era explains the Geheime Feldpolizei euphemistically as "a special troop for security, independent of the regular military units". Let me first say that they were men in military uniform, but really "employees" of the Gestapo, operating officially under the command of the German Military Intelligence. Their highest ranking commander was a personal friend of the infamous Heydrich who had given these people their training.

They committed many crimes, especially in the occupied East European countries where they were either functioning as single units or as part of death squads.

Why they were called "secret" never became clear to me because, besides being highly visible in their uniforms, they also wore silver breast-plates, held by chains around their necks. German soldiers gave them the nickname "Kettenhunde" (chain-dogs).

We still could not get a clear picture of the military situation and, at the time, it remained too risky to escape. Preparing an escape plan is like fine-tuning a clock. Only after looking over everything from different angles and considering which moves will provide the best chances for optimum results, can sound decisions be made.

Now, I have to introduce you to Alfred, who was also of Jewish origin. He did not belong to the Plauen circle, but had impressed me by his spirit of initiative. He was a reliable type of chap, the kind with whom one can go through thick and thin.

When I began thinking about escape, I realized that I did not want to make my getaway with a whole bunch of inmates, yet I did not want to go by myself. A small team of two seemed best to me and who appeared to be more qualified than Alfred?

Then came Thursday morning, June 8th. We had stayed in camp all the time, and had not seen Otf. Leutner; only his deputy. We had not been ordered to do anything special. Some prisoners were assigned to the cleaning crew, and that was all.

Around 9:00 a.m., a terrible bombardment rained hundreds of bombs on Valognes, destroying the centre of the town, including the main church and, extremely close to our camp, a row of houses with a corner bookstore. No attempt was made to hold us back in the camp anymore. Alfred and I looked at the site where the bookstore had been. The ruins were smouldering and beams were still burning, when we heard a muffled voice.

Three or four Frenchmen were digging and gesticulating

and, as we came closer, we heard faint cries from underneath the debris. It turned out that a girl was lying under the ruins, still alive. [19] Her mother was dead on top of her. We jumped into the hole, tried to help to remove, as fast as possible, the debris from the two bodies, and with combined strength we partially succeeded. Yet, when we reached the girl, her awareness and pain seemed to become more acute and she let out a scream which shook us to the core. Smoke from the fire made us cough. One large and cracked wall of the house was still standing and threatened to collapse onto us at any moment, but still we all kept digging.

In spite of our hard work, we were unable to free the girl, because a huge beam had jammed her. This beam had also saved her life, as it had prevented the debris from crushing her to death.

We reached her with water but, as she gained more consciousness, she started screaming again, most probably because of pain, shock and fear.

In the meantime, drawn and pushed by people, a piece of fire-fighting equipment had arrived but, since it was impossible to make it work, the smouldering fire could not be extinguished. We continued working.

All of a sudden, SS-forces passed by on the street. Two camp guards spotted us working in the slow-burning ruin. They brandished their pistols and shouted that we should hurry and come back to the prison camp. We really had no choice but to return. Some other prisoners who had tried to escape had already been caught and nothing good was in store for them. Others had left the camp with armed guards and returned with them.

Otf. Leutner decided we should all leave Valognes immediately, and so we had to pack our few belongings and within minutes march off towards Bricquebec. On the road we were stopped by a messenger, a soldier on a motorcycle, who announced that the General (I have forgotten the name.) expected volunteers for the German Armed Forces. Most of the prisoners refused to enlist, but some felt that they would have a better chance to survive and to get out of the whole mess if they did.

**Valognes. View with Church before 1944
and destroyed church after bombardments**

Among those was Dr. Walter U. and a short, stocky fellow, a butcher by trade.

After the war, I learned that Walter had been lucky and survived. He had been captured by the Americans and, ironically, had to spend time as a prisoner-of-war in a POW camp in the USA. Yet, he was one of the first to be released after the war ended. The butcher was killed in a battle. They had received German uniforms without insignia of rank, were told in an afternoon instruction course how to fire a rifle, and that was it.

Poldi, Alfred and I had discussed the situation in detail. We knew that the Germans were desperate to reinforce their defence troops. Why should we, who were hoping the Allies would end the war and liberate us soon, support the Nazis?

There was another, though only theoretical consideration. Should, heaven forbid, the Allied invasion be unsuccessful, all prisoners who had volunteered and risked their lives for "Führer and Reich" would have to go back into slave labour and concentration camps, only to be killed in the end.

On a different road, we then marched back to the outskirts of Valognes where Otf. Leutner sent his deputy ahead to confiscate a farmhouse with a barn across the road leading from Valognes to Cherbourg. [20]

The armed guards took turns watching over the prisoners who were jammed into the barn. Leutner moved into the farmhouse with his staff. He was really scared about the whole situation and began drinking more than ever. While in a sort of semi-stupor, he kept an old, ugly whore in his bedroom all the time. Her skin was so shrivelled, it looked like the gill lining of a mushroom. When Leutner came out of the room, which happened only rarely, one could see that he was only a shadow of his former self. He was unkempt, had a violetish face, parts of his uniform were unbuttoned and his collar was dirty; he staggered in an atmosphere of alcohol while his Baltic Cross dangled from the ribbon around his neck. Without doubt, he was well-stocked with liquor because he had sent a couple of criminals into Valognes, where they must have pillaged a restaurant or bar.

How do I know all this? Otf. Leutner did not trust his first-aider, the criminal, anymore. When he had chosen him, he did not care about the prisoners this criminal would treat, because they "did not deserve any better". Now he was looking for somebody who, in an emergency situation, would take care of him and the woman. Since Walter U., the physician, was already in the German Army, I volunteered as first-aid man, thinking of many eventual possibilities. Above all, I was allowed to sleep and stay in the farmhouse, which meant not being guarded and also being allowed certain liberties.

We knew that the Pharmacy Lemarquand in Valognes had been destroyed the same day as the Bookstore Brochard. Realizing that certain material could probably still be saved before weather or new bombing made it useless, I suggested to Leutner that I go into town and get a few things for our first-aid supply. When he welcomed this suggestion, I quickly added that I could not do this by myself. From this moment on, Alfred was also a "member of the farmhouse staff", as I had planned it. We went into Valognes, to the Rue des Religieuses, and picked up a few bandages and medications which were lying around. When we returned, Leutner, staring at me with his red, glassy eyes, roared because I had not immediately reported back from Valognes and did not stand at attention. This may sound harmless and unimportant, but Leutner, in his state of fear and uncertainty, was a time bomb which could have exploded at any minute and, as we will see, he did so not too much later.

Among the items we had brought back was a bottle of brandy which we had found among the rubble of the pharmacy. I wanted to keep it for emergency cases. However, it was amazing how quickly Otf. Leutner spotted this bottle and grabbed it for his own consumption. When I mentioned that we might need the brandy as a tonic for a wounded person, he began cursing and swearing, reached for his pistol in his holster and barked at me to shut up or I would get a bullet through my head. Knowing Leutner only too well, I immediately kept quiet while he, once again, retired upstairs to his tart for his four standard activities:

boozing, fornicating, eating and sleeping.

In a ground-floor corner of a room in the farmhouse we then established our first-aid post.

Together with another prisoner, who had been elected Leutner's servant, we now received the same food as Leutner and the guards. This was by no means a minor advantage. Ordered by Leutner, the servant not only had to bring him and the woman food, but also he had to be outside the bedroom door at all times waiting for Leutner's instructions, handing him his uniform cap whenever he left the room and performing all kinds of other lackey services.

The guards became more friendly and tried to fraternize because, by then, they had a pretty good idea what things would be like if we were overrun by Allied forces. But, as can be expected, we gave them the cold shoulder.

I remember that there was another bombardment of Valognes in the evening twilight yet, when I inquired after the war, nobody mentioned another air-raid on June 8th. Whatever, it eventually became dark and quiet. Once in a while a car passed on the road. The general silence was like the lull before a storm. Something was brewing, and somehow, the suspense was not only because of the Landing as such, but also our anxiety about what would happen during the following days.

The "watchdogs" who were not on guard slept in beds. Alfred and I were lying downstairs on the hard, wooden floor but, although dog-tired, were too excited to fall asleep right away. We must have dozed off later, because we were suddenly roused by somebody rumbling down the stairs. We heard the shrill screaming of the Otf., then a bang and a thud. From then on, total silence.

Quite bewildered, we got up and tried to find out what had happened. We heard Leutner snapping: "This swine disturbed me; he had to be bumped off."

In front of the house lay a dark mass. I checked and he was dead. At this moment Leutner yelled again: "That body stays on the ground until every one of you has seen him, exactly as he is: d-e-a-d!"

The dangerous "time bomb had detonated.

What had happened? One of the prisoners, a Gypsy, had been sent by a guard from the barn to report something. Since the door of the farmhouse was locked, he had knocked on the door (which we had not heard). For this alone, he was shot.

Neither the night nor the trouble had ended. The prisoner-servant, who had to remain at Leutner's bedroom door all the time to hand him his uniform cap, had a nervous breakdown. It was probably the constant stress as a prisoner, the bombardments, the tension during recent days, over-fatigue and, now, the murder of a fellow prisoner that brought him to breaking point. He began to scream like a madman, threw the Otf.'s uniform cap away, kicked a chair so that it broke and raged like a lunatic.

As one, Alfred and I jumped up, threw ourselves on him, subdued him, and stuffed something into his mouth. After we had dragged him down the stairs, Alfred sat on him while I gave him a strong sedative. I am certain that we saved him, and maybe even ourselves, from being shot by Leutner.

Again silence. And again it did not last long. The energy-consuming activity with Leutner, the events of the night, and surely, also, her prospects of being treated as collaborator by her fellow citizens once the Germans had gone, caused the Otf.'s woman to crack up. She started whimpering and wailing. Leutner foamed. Alfred and I were afraid that there might be another blood bath because the constantly drunken Leutner no longer had the least bit of self-control, if, indeed, he had ever had any. He was a loose cannon. Then morning was dawning. This seemed to have a generally sobering, soothing effect which took away some of the anxieties of the night.

At the morning roll-call on the road, in front of the farmhouse, everybody had to look at the dead man who was lying in a pool of blood. Some got sick, two passed out. After the guards had marched the prisoners back to the barn, the Otf. cried for his "quasi-sawbones", became hysterical and waved his heavy pistol under my nose. He ordered me to bury the dead man within half an hour, anywhere at all, and no excuses. Standing at attention this time in order not to irritate him, I said with a loud voice a snappy "Jawohl!" He always liked this kind of military behaviour. I did not. But, on the other hand, I realized that one had to make certain concessions in order to stay alive. Deep inside I felt anything but snappy, mostly because I was just as much afraid of him becoming sober and having a hangover as I was scared of him being drunk. I made an about-turn and dashed out of his sight.

Nowhere could I find a pickax or a spade. After a while, I found a shovel with a long handle behind the farmhouse. With this tool, however, one could not dig even five centimetres deep into the hard soil in half an hour. Then I looked for any sort of cart to transport the body somewhere in the direction of Valognes, hoping to find a more suitable place with softer soil there. At the barn, on the other side of the road, I found a wheelbarrow. Calling Alfred, I asked him to help me lift the corpse onto the push cart. As soon as he looked at the dead man, he lamented and refused to touch him. Even telling him that we risked being shot ourselves if we did not remove this body did not bring him to his senses. I believed Leutner capable of doing the worst and was so scared that I tried to heave the lifeless body onto the wheelbarrow myself, but did not succeed because the cart always tipped over and the corpse slipped. This made more blood ooze out of the wound. At this moment Alfred fainted.

Precious time had already been lost. After I had brought dear Alfred around, I rushed to the barn, said to the guard that by order of Otf. Leutner I was to select a helper for the burial of the dead Gypsy, and chose a tall, burly, red-haired man from Dresden. We laid the poor dead fellow on a blanket, grasped the four corners, lifted him onto the wheelbarrow and carted him off down the road, leaving a trail of blood where we walked because the wheelbarrow had a crack at the bottom.

We checked left and right to find a suitable place with soft soil, but in vain. The bitter fact was we could not dig a grave anywhere. As we kept looking, we suddenly noticed two square holes in the ground not far from a farmhouse. [21] Were they two graves prepared for burial, or were they two slit shelter trenches the size of graves? We did not lose time with contemplating and philosophizing about the intended purpose of the trenches, but carted the dead man to one of these holes and lowered him as respectfully as possible into the ground. Unfortunately, the blanket was not large enough to cover the body completely, and we felt it would have been irreverent to simply throw earth on the man's face. So we placed some leaves on his face, and then took turns shovelling loose soil from the mound beside the opening into the grave.

We assumed that this Gypsy from East Prussia, father of four children, had been of the Christian faith. Not far from the trees under which this trench or grave had been dug, was an abandoned horse carriage left by the German military. We tore off two boards. My red-haired companion brought two nails, and we set up a makeshift cross at the head of the grave. After each of us had said a silent prayer for the dead man, we rushed back to report to Otf. Leutner that we had carried out his orders, being sure that he had already been looking at his watch.

Years later, I visited Valognes and inquired about the grave. The farmers living in this particular farmhouse told me that, in this grave, quite near the surface and covered with only a little soil, they had found a German soldier in 1944. He had then been transferred to the war cemetery. Obviously, they did not realize there was another body underneath. This would be quite reasonable to assume, since we had been unable to fill the grave completely. Consequently, there was still an approximately seventy centimetres deep opening on top of the person we had buried. Also, the soil that we had shovelled into the grave may have settled somewhat, which then created the impression that nothing was in the grave below the body which was found.

The people promised they would notify the German War Graves Commission. Whether or not any action was really taken, I do not know as nobody ever contacted me afterwards.

6. — Background Information

As already mentioned, the weather in May 1944 was beautiful. Based on factors such as tides, moon, etc., Allied meteorologists calculated the 5th, 6th or 7th of June, 1944 to be the most suitable dates for an invasion of France. But since nature runs pretty much its own course, it is hardly possible to give completely reliable weather information more than a day or two in advance, and weather was certainly a crucial factor for such a gigantic cross-Channel operation. At the end, in fact, the go-ahead hinged almost solely on the weather. The first days of June were marked by rough seas because of gale-force winds, rain and low clouds in the Channel and over large parts of the Atlantic. The weather was so bad that even German Field marshal Rommel, who was more or less the only top-ranking general who expected the invasion to take place on Normandy shores, was convinced that a landing operation would not be possible under such conditions. He decided to drive home to Germany, not only because he was exhausted, but also because the 6th of June was his wife's fiftieth birthday.

Even though the bad weather had an awfully negative influence on the great landing, which had already been postponed one day from its original target date for the offensive, it had its positive side, too. Most of the German commanding and staff-officers stationed in Normandy were not worried about an invasion. They went to the city of Rennes for a war exercise meeting. Also, the Germans had cancelled all of their air and sea activities because of the bad weather. Working hard and continuously, the Allied meteorologists could predict a short break with improved weather for the 6th. This in the end induced US General Eisenhower's decision to attack. The 6th of June 1944 became D-Day.

On Y-Day, which had the codename Halcyon, all preparations for the landing had to be completed. June 1st was chosen to be that day.

We find many such code names throughout the war. The assault phase of operation Overlord, the Allied Invasion of France, was called Neptune, and H-Hour stood for the hour of landing of Allied troops on Normandy shores.

As it was mentioned before, the Allies had planted misinformation about the actual area of landing. This was an ingenious deception in connection with operation Overlord but cannot be told here in its details. One can find pertinent literature on the fascinating intelligence preparations for the diversionary attacks on the Pas-de-Calais area in most libraries. This action was called, very appropriately "Operation Bodyguard", because it safeguarded the actual Invasion to a great extend.

In contrast to Rommel, Hitler and his High Command believed initially that the actual Normandy invasion was only a diversionary manoeuvre. Because of this, they left main troop concentrations in other regions of France, so as to be able to counter what they expected would then be the real invasion. There was of course a good reason for this decision. The Germans had been fooled before and were now afraid of crying wolf. If by chance anyone gave a false alarm, alerting everybody for nothing, they would bring even more unrest among the troops.

We had been wondering about the swarms of airplanes flying over Valognes. Allied pilots flew 25,000 sorties on D-Day, dropping 12,000 tons of bombs, compared to only approximately 100 sorties by the Germans. It was indeed a mammoth operation. Almost 5000 ships left England that night. The American air strength alone came close to 13,000 planes, of which 4500 were big bombers.

The heavy bombing in the first stages of the invasion, carried out mostly by medium bombers, was calculated to hit the coastal regions first and then the lines of supply and possible reinforcement, as well as railway junctions and bridges. Thin strips of tinfoil, such as had been used during air-raids on German cities after 1943, were dropped to confuse German radar reception.

The second stage of the invasion was to drop paratroopers of the 82nd and 101st American Paratroop Division into the zone between Ste. Mère-Eglise (seventeen kilometres from Valognes) and Carentan. Then, after making contact with the troops of the US VII Corps' 4th Infantry Division, who were to be landed on Utah Beach (This code name designated a particular section of the Allied landing area.), the plan was to cut off the German forces at the neck of the Cotentin peninsula. Utah Beach was not more than twelve kilometres away from Valognes, as the crow flies.

The paratroopers jumped from DC-3s and other airborne troops were landed with gliders, mostly between 1:00 and 3:00 a.m., but the entire operation from the air lasted well into the dawn hours. Unfortunately, the high winds which still prevailed scattered paratroopers about and some drifted as much as fifty-five kilometres off their target. Cherbourg measured a wind force of seven on the Beaufort Scale that night.

The troop transport super-gliders, approximately 3500 of them, were pulled by planes and connected by towing cables.

The Rommel Asparagus with mines attached to their tops presented deadly obstacles for the airborne division, gliders and men, but equally so did the natural environment with hedgerows, trees and flooded areas. Together they caused many terrible losses. A great number of soldiers, for instance, landed in swamps or flooded fields and drowned because they were not able to free themselves, in time, of the heavy equipment they carried.

Dummy paratroopers, with either fire crackers attached or with devices which exploded on impact, were dropped and caused considerable confusion among the Germans. Some of them made the sound of automatic weapons, and others released smoke or even gave off a smell typical of combat. From the distance, and particularly in the dark, they looked like real combat troopers, and quite an amount of shooting was directed on these dummies. It took a while until messages about this diversionary trick got through to the German command posts and headquarters.

On June 6th, 1944 at 7:25 a.m., the third stage of joint operations, the amphibious landing, followed.

By midnight, more than 150,000 men had been landed. It has to be mentioned here that, of the Allied troops who were killed in action on D-Day, ten percent were Jewish, while the proportion of the Jewish people in the USA is approximately 1% of the total population.

The German General von Schlieben was ordered to breach through the US landing area and take Ste. Mère-Eglise, which had already been seized by the US 505th Parachute Infantry Regiment. However, for a multitude of reasons the German attack could not be accomplished as ordered. Another offensive, which was started off in the evening hours, was beaten back by the US paratroopers. Also all of the left flank of the LXXXIV Corps of the German 7th Army in the Ste. Mère-Eglise area was defeated. [22]

The Allies were unable to advance quickly because of the obstacles the country itself offered. For instance, the hedgerows. On the one hand, they gave welcome protection for the landed troops but, on the other hand, they also provided convenient tactical coverage for the Germans.

The "prairies marécageuses" (swampy marshlands) and their canals were flooded by the Germans and, therefore, became double jeopardy for men and their vehicles.

On top of all that, the US forces had to separate their units in order to drive their attacks north towards Cherbourg as well as south-east to St. Lô, with the final aim being to cut off the Germans on the Cotentin peninsula, as mentioned before.

Because, initially, no continuous Allied front line existed, only many so-called hedgehog positions, our escape plans met with considerable difficulties. Details about the consideration of our escape problems will be explained later.

Only on June 18th, 1944, after having gradually narrowed the neck, could the Allies finally break through to the west coast of the peninsula, and so isolate Cherbourg.

It took another month to gain just ten to twenty kilometres of territory. A real thrust into the German lines began only in the middle of August and, with that, the first phase of the Allied mobile warfare began.

— June 25th, 1944 — Allied troops entered Cherbourg. — June 28th, 1944 — The Cherbourg fortress capitulated. — June 30th, 1944 — The whole Cotentin peninsula was in Allied hands. — August 1st, 1944 — US troops break through at Avranche, which enabled them to penetrate into the Bretagne.

The record shows that there was hardly any coordination or cooperation between the German Armed Forces — Army, Navy and Air Force. Even Field marshal Gerd von Rundstaedt, the Commander-in-Chief of the Western Command, had no authority to organize any joint action, much to the advantage of the invading Allies. Hitler, as the Supreme Commander, was afraid to delegate too much authority to any one of his generals, ruled by the principle of "divide et impera!" (Divide and rule!) He avoided having an authoritative centralized system below him as he feared a military conspiracy and coup.

SS and Gestapo controlled all non-military matters inside occupied France. We learn from official sources that only by chance did von Rundstedt get knowledge of their activities.

In France or the West, it would have only been logical to have one person decide what was necessary to be done in this situation, but this would have required a coordinated effort, which simply did not exist in the German situation. There was no structured line of command in the higher echelons. Nobody in the upper German military hierarchy really knew who was doing what. Hitler, possessed by megalomania, believed he was the greatest strategist of all time. Precisely because of this, he kept the branches of the German military forces apart. This disorganization was one of the major reasons why Germany was finally defeated.

If we had known at the time, of course, we prisoners of the SS and Gestapo would have been delighted about such organizational chaos within the German war machinery. The more, the better!

7. — The Escape

Alfred and I were now in the farmhouse and practically unguarded. Occasionally, we saw SS drive by outside. Half of the unit of criminals who had replaced the OT-guards were in the barn watching over all of the other prisoners; the other half was sleeping. Leutner's deputy either joined the guards in the barn or was sleeping at the same time as the off-duty men. Therefore, the circumstances for an escape were reasonably good.

The thought of escape had been on our minds for quite some time but, in the past weeks and days, the situation had been very unfavourable. This had changed now. Still, there were many problems. After the War, I was often asked why we did not simply take off and run over to the Allied troops. We did not for the following reasons:

a) We would have had to cross through territory occupied by the German Army and the SS, both of whom were very suspicious of civilians moving about in the war zone. Such people could, for instance, be men from the Resistance (Maquisards) or Jedburghs (explanation will follow later). There were strict controls, despite the general confusion. Secret Field Police and SS were all over the area.

b) If caught trying to escape to the Allies, we would have been shot on the spot. No questions asked. No trial. No defence. This was common practice when Martial Law was in effect.

c) There would be a considerable risk in crossing the fire lines. One had a good chance of being shot either in the front or in the back.

d) After their airborne landing, the US troops established scattered defence emplacements, so-called hedgehog positions. In other words, there was no continuous defence line. Even if we had been incredibly lucky and reached such a position, we could not have been sure that the Germans would not retake the site. If they did, even if only temporarily, the Americans would go to a POW camp and we would, without any hesitation, be shot.

At this point in time, not even military strategists were absolutely sure that the invasion would succeed as planned. The Germans hoped it would be a second Dunkirk. Furthermore, we knew only that there was an invasion. Whether or not it was the actual offensive, or merely a diversionary manoeuvre, was not at all clear. Sometimes, the tides of war change very quickly.

e) Knowing that there were not only many patriotic, anti-German French people but also most likely, the same number of collaborators and informers, it would have been impossible for us to contact just any French person, hoping that they would get us in touch with the Resistance. Who was friend and who was foe?

Whoever considers these essential points will understand that the risk factor with such an ill-considered, simple take-off strategy was much too great. Therefore, we decided, at least for the time being, to escape away from the battle areas, towards the inner part of France until the Allies could consolidate an actual front line.

The off-duty guards had leaned their rifles against a wall inside the farmhouse. In one corner, Otf. Leutner had even stored hand-grenades. Should we take some to throw them on the farmhouse or not? The temptation was great, but our fear even greater. An explosion in or out of the house would have immediately attracted SS and army troops, and our escape chances would have been reduced to practically zero.

Therefore, one morning, when the guards from the barn had just been relieved and had gone to sleep, Alfred and I went quietly out of the house and ran like crazy until we reached a crossroads to the Route Nationale, which branched off to Bricquebec. Each of us had a bag and a blanket. In each bag were some provisions and a pair of new leather boots, which we had stolen from the storage room of the camp before we had left to use them as bartering commodities.

After we had walked a few kilometres, we burned all of our identification papers, except the admission pass for the construction site, the only document which did not show our Jewish

Author's escape route through France

descent. Everybody, including the guards, had the same type of clearance paper which was renewed each month with a special stamp. We did not realize then that destroying our real identification papers would prove almost fatal in the near future.

We did not go into the village of Bricquebec but turned left to St. Sauveur-le-Vicomte. After we had left this town behind us, Allied fighter bombers attacked. They not only strafed German positions, but shot at almost everything that moved along Route Nationale N800 with cannons and machine guns. They even dropped small bombs. From then on, we moved about 2.5 meters for each meter of road. Why? The road was elevated, with low ditches left and right. As an aircraft approached from one side, we jumped into the opposite ditch and pressed ourselves as close as possible against the wall to shield us from the bullets. Then as the aircraft turned, we had to jump into the other ditch.

N800 was, at that time, the only highway on the Cotentin peninsula not cut off by the Allies. Their planes were ever present to prevent any German supply vehicles or troop-and-weapon reinforcements from reaching front lines. Such attacks got even worse between La Haye-du-Puits and Lessay. It was really a cat-and-mouse game with us and, since we were the mice, we did not find it very amusing.

Between these two communities, we met a German bicycle unit. In a modern war, it was very strange to see soldiers pushing their bicycles, but one must remember that Germany was on her last legs. The very young and friendly lieutenant in charge asked us something in French. When I told him we could speak German, he was extremely surprised. Then we rolled off our story about being German civilian workers who were escaping from the invasion area, and had to leave all our personal belongings behind. For some reason the lieutenant seemed to be happy to talk with somebody who was not a "G.I. Joe", because he said quite openly that he envied us for being able to go away from the fighting zone. He even said how crazy it was to order him and his men to go by bicycle to Cherbourg, since the war could not be won by Germany anyhow.

Alfred and I looked at each other because what the officer had just said was an act of treason under the Nazi regime. Defeatism was a crime, considered "Wehrkraft-Zersetzung" (demoralization of the military). He could have been court-martialed and executed for this.

His men seemed equally opposed to the idea of pushing both their bicycles and their luck. We finally had to part and wished both the lieutenant and his men good health.

Statistics show that, from November 1943 to January 1944, 23,000 bicycles were furnished to the German army units in France. Furthermore, even ancient French bicycles had been requisitioned for military use. The 709th Infantry Division had horses and mules to move their equipment and weapons.

Predictably, German troop morale was very low. Not only had the war already lasted many years, but it had also become increasingly clear to German soldiers that they were only cannon fodder for Hitler.

In a quiet moment, we sat down and discussed our situation. We had escaped, but also realized that the more we got away from the hot spots, the less the confusion and, therefore, the greater our chances of falling into the net of tight German controls. We were quite sure that, no matter what their personal feelings towards Jews were, the people we could rely on most for not giving us away would be priests. We began to call on every parsonage on our way, explaining our predicament and asking to be hidden until the Americans occupied this area. We were never successful.

Alan Moorehead says in his book, ECLIPSE: "Whenever our patrols or our airmen got cut off, they were sure of finding someone to hide them in the first farmhouse they visited." It did not work for us but, remember, we were not readily identifiable as escaped prisoners of the Germans, and therefore were probably always suspected of being "agents provocateurs". Also, who wanted to risk his skin shortly before the liberation? In hindsight, this behaviour seems to be very logical but, at the time of our escape, we were rather disappointed and frustrated by what we thought was a cold attitude.

On the other hand, it must be stated that we were always permitted to sleep in a barn and always got at least some food, no matter how little may have been available. For this, we could consider ourselves lucky. We learned later that the French Maquisards killed Germans while they slept, cutting their throats or knifing them. While we were sleeping in the barns, relatively unconcerned and carefree, they could easily have mistaken us for German civilians, which in a sense we were, and killed us. Happily, this possibility never entered our minds, because we felt only threatened by the people from our own country.

It seems that, in these first days of the invasion, there was hardly any contact between the villages on the Cotentin peninsula. We bartered our boots for butter, and received at least seven to eight pounds each. Then, in another village where they were short on butter, we exchanged some of ours for bread. It was as if each village lived in isolation.

It was late, almost dark, when we came to a farmhouse between Lessay and Coutances, near Muneville. To our surprise the people in this farmhouse spoke English and we could therefore communicate with them much better than with the French. It turned out that they had been evacuated by the Germans from the Island of Jersey. Immediately, we were invited to sleep there and eat with them. What a reception! Wine, bread, butter, fried fish, and a warm, friendly atmosphere. We all sat around the table, with parents and children, eating and talking. They said that Carentan was completely destroyed and still burning. Those good people would have hidden us but, as evacuees from an English Island they were suspects themselves, especially now that the English, together with the Americans, had invaded the Continent. They expected that very soon they, too, would have to leave the approaching battle zone, as well as their property.

When it was time to retire, they insisted that we use their beds and they slept in the straw. Their kindness was just unbelievable. Because Alfred and I were so tired and were sleeping in real beds for a change, we initially heard nothing of the night attack on the nearby main road. Only when the farmer came and woke us up did we hear the exploding bombs and firing of aircraft weapons, cannons and machine guns. Not knowing whether or not the assault would be confined to the road area, the farmer suggested that we all move to the close-by moor land for a while. His wife and the children were already waiting.

Naturally, the Germans tried to move supplies and reinforcements under cover of night and it was not difficult for the Allies to anticipate such actions. It must have been more than an hour later when everything calmed down and we returned to the farmhouse. We went back to bed and, in the morning, had a hearty breakfast. When the two of us parted from the Jersey people, we thanked them from the bottom of our hearts and wished them lots of good luck for the future. We all needed this luck. In the muddle of events, we forgot to ask them for their names, which I sincerely regret to this day. My inquiries after the war were without any positive results.

Once in a while Alfred and I disagreed on which way we should go. While Alfred said it was safer to take field paths, I maintained that this would make us look suspicious. Being plain noticeable, we would be less conspicuous. Moreover, it would be faster and, therefore, preferable to take the main roads. This we did.

Shortly before noon we saw three tanks standing on the road. The crew, in shirt sleeves, was approximately thirty meters away playing cards. They were SS-men, probably from the 12th SS-Panzer Division. They called us and waved us to come over. When we asked them jokingly why they were playing cards and not moving in their tanks, they said: "Do you think we are crazy? Our tanks will be destroyed anyway. Better let them be destroyed with us rushing into the fields, than with us sitting inside." We could not believe such words coming from SS, but were highly pleased at the evidently declining morale of even the elite troops of Nazi Germany.

We came into the town of Coutances, which was almost totally destroyed. As we passed through ruins, seeing only a few people, we came upon a bombed-out bicycle shop. Although we saw only wire skeletons from a distance, we hoped that there might still be usable bike parts which we would have assembled. While we were standing there and looking, two men ran toward us, shaking their fists and screaming at us. It did not take us long to leave.

A German Red Cross truck with wounded soldiers stood outside of town ready to leave. We asked the driver whether he would be so kind to give us a ride. After some hesitation, he agreed but stipulated we were not to look out from under the canvas cover if aircraft were above us. It had happened, he said, that, when soldiers had opened the tarpaulin and either peeked out or even left the truck, Allied planes had started shooting at them.

He admitted, though, that, in some cases, German Red Cross vehicles had been used to bring reinforcements and ammunition to the front. This, of course, was strictly against the international regulations of the Geneva Convention.

Only too glad to give our legs and feet a rest, we consented and mounted the truck. When we tried to start a conversation with the soldiers, we found that they could not speak German. They were Russians or Ukrainians. Later the driver's mate explained that rather than being POW's in one of the many German camps with intolerable living conditions and a starvation diet, these foreigners had volunteered to join the so-called East Troops. In March 1944, there had been 61,500 such volunteers. Unbelievable as it may sound, these "unreliables"; as the Germans called them, formed over fifteen percent of the LXXXIV Corps. Many, if not most of them, were in the 795th Georgian and the 642nd Ost (East) Battalion.

German military units, which had been thinned out by a war dragging on and on, were also restocked by "Volksdeutsche" (Ethnic Germans) from occupied countries, independently from the aforementioned volunteers who were not Ethnic Germans. Strangely enough, or perhaps not so strangely, the Nazis did not mind these "subhumans and racially intolerables", as they had

Mortain. "L'Abbaye Blanche" now.
It was used as a German Field Hospital in 1944.

classified them, risking their hides for the Greater German Empire. It was a means to an end.

Furthermore, a significant part of the German Army on the Western Front consisted of German invalids from the eastern front. All of this was of benefit to the Allies.

It came as no surprise to us when Allied aircraft suddenly appeared. Our truck stopped and the driver, a lance corporal (US Army equivalent: private 1st class) ordered everybody to remain on their seats. I must say, it was not very pleasant sitting there hoping not to be shot at. In my imagination, I saw the canvas riddled by bullets, looking like Swiss cheese. Four times the fighter-bombers flew extremely low over us, as if they wanted to peek inside the truck. Then they took off. Maybe the fact that we were driving away from the War Zone, rather than towards it, had saved our lives.

The truck went on and stopped in front of a German field hospital in Mortain. It used to be an abbey and seminary, L'Abbaye Blanche, out of which the Institut Notre-Dame in Avranches had developed. [23]

Because of the ongoing battles, there were many wounded soldiers to be looked after. A great number of army medical corps personnel had been ordered to front line duty, and there was a drastic shortage of hospital orderlies. We said that, although we had to go back to Paris eventually to report to our construction company (which of course was a fat lie), seeing the present shortage of people, we would be prepared to stay for a few days and help out, providing we could get accommodation and meals.

The chief surgeon was quite happy with such an arrangement and did not ask any awkward questions. His duty was to help the wounded and the dying, not to support the fighting or to enforce certain Nazi rules and regulations.

For three full days we worked as orderlies in this hospital, which in peace time was occupied by the Frères de Saint Esprit who spent most of their time preparing missionaries from and for Africa.

We left the field hospital at Mortain on a cloudy day, which

**Domfront, in 1994(above), and in 1944 after the bombardment
(photos with kind authorization of Monsieur Gilles Susong)**

had a depressing effect on our psyches, even though we had had a good breakfast. We were happy that there was no disturbance from the air because we were tired of the jumping game: left ditch/right ditch. Each of us mused about something while we were trotting along. Then we saw the picturesque town of Domfront ahead of us, lying there on the slope of a hill. Right in front of us was a railroad crossing. Suddenly, as we reached this level crossing, we heard the noise of aircraft and, at the same time, saw them as they came nose-diving for an assault. We had had no more than two or three seconds to leap over to the left into a hollow way, when the bombs started dropping. Explosion after explosion came in rapid succession. Rocks, soil, and pieces of metal were flying all about. The air pressure pushed us against the ground and it was hard to breathe. Everything was enveloped in a huge cloud of dust. [23]

We were lucky nothing happened to us. Fortunately, the level crossing was not in a very populated area and nobody had been hurt. Now that the planes had met their objective and bombed the crossing to smithereens, we thought it would become quiet enough for us to take our time and stroll through town, looking leisurely at houses on the main street. Not so. We had barely come three-quarters of the way through the town when we again heard the sound of aircraft. This time the noise indicated heavy bombers. We ran and ran as fast as our feet would carry us. As we threw ourselves behind a thick hedge next to a farmhouse, heavy bombs rained on Domfront. Dense, dark, and sometimes black smoke, mixed with yellow-orange flames, rose up, producing a sooty fall-out which gradually settled over the whole terrain. We wondered how many people must have died or been wounded. Most of Domfront was in ruins.

Looking at things from a strategic point of view, the bombing should not have surprised us, because cutting off the one and only Route Nationale on the Cotentin peninsula still in German hands was now the goal of the Allies, and Domfront was located on the crossing of N162 and N807. The road designations may be different nowadays.

**Domfront city boundary (above - at present) and
Domfront after 1944 bombardment. (With kind permission of Gilles Susong)**

There was a bus on the road, packed with SS-men, four or five kilometres outside Domfront. Some of these black-uniformed Germans were just getting on. Applying the saying "Better to have an uncomfortable ride than go on foot," we had the nerve to ask the driver if he would let us get on, too. We gave them the old spiel about German civilian workers trying to return to their construction company in Paris. And so "the inferior race persons" rode on a bus with "the German SS Master Race." If they had only known! Anyway, this got us into the region of Alençon.

Somehow, it is in my mind that we stayed in a barn in Neufchatel overnight, but I cannot find such a name on the map now.

The next day, between Alençon and Bellême, we ran into a trap. [24] The road went through a sort of ravine. Behind a bend, a road-block had been set up. Left and right were slopes, which meant it was impossible to climb up and escape unnoticed. We simply had to continue on the road. There was a barrier and a guardhouse with a table outside. One German soldier controlled the traffic, letting certain vehicles pass and stopping others. Passengers had to show identification papers. Another soldier was sweeping the surroundings with binoculars.

There was already a line-up in front of the table, where an army sergeant together with an OT-Scharführer, or Truppführer, checked credentials. Listening to the conversations in front of us, we heard that a lot of soldiers maintained they were stragglers, separated from their units. Alfred and I could not imagine that they had all been scattered at the Invasion Front, and come all the way beyond Alençon without finding an army unit or a collecting point to which to report. It was standard procedure that such soldiers had to report to the next available army unit. Therefore, we were convinced that most of them were actually deserters who had had enough of fighting, with the likelihood of dying or being wounded.

Naturally, our real worries were not with these soldiers. There was no easy way out of this for us, and we had to face the music. When our turn came at the table, we gave them the old story about German civilian workers, etc. Why did we have only construction site passes, they asked. "We were taken by surprise when the invasion came, and were at the construction site with only this admission pass. Our real identification papers were destroyed during a bombing raid, together with our other personal belongings," we replied.

This was neither very logical nor very believable, but at the time it was all we could come up with. Another armed OT-man, in typical olive green uniform with a swastika armlet, escorted us to a nearby camp located in the woods, for further scrutiny.

When we arrived at the guardhouse, we were handed over to the guard. The escort man left and the guard went to the telephone. Alfred and I signalled each other with our eyes, and like lightening we dived into the adjoining woods, in which a dense fern cover grew under the trees. We heard the guard screaming and people coming, talking loudly. There must have been a search party after us, but we did not dare to take the time to turn around and look. Surrounded by ferns like jungle growth, we crawled as carefully as possible so as not to leave a visible path. I do not know how long we moved on our hands and knees, one behind the other, but when we finally stopped to catch our breath, we were bruised all over from broken tree branches and rocks on the ground. We thought it would be wise to spend the night under the dense ferns in the wood. We had our blankets alright, but the ground was moist and rather uncomfortable in spite of the soft moss.

The next morning greeted us with beautiful sunshine. We were very hungry because we had not had a bite since noon the previous day. We avoided the main road for quite some distance, making our way with difficulty through the pathless brushwood. As we came closer to the road, the woods opened up and we saw a lovely sunlit meadow spread out in front of us. To our surprise, we found a plenitude of wild strawberries. We must have sat there for almost an hour eating strawberries which, incidentally, had a fantastic aroma. Everything around us was quiet and peaceful.

The air was balmy. After the hectic days filled with bombing, shooting, running, and the constant fear of being apprehended, this was like paradise, and an old poem which my mother had frequently recited came to my mind:
"*Quand la nature est reverdie, Quand l'hirondelle est de retour, J'aime à revoir ma Normandie . . .* "
God willing, one day I would be back, when the sun would shine again over a peaceful France and tranquil Normandy. [24]

We came through Nogent-le-Rotrou and approached Chartres. This time it was Alfred who wanted to go on the main road right through the town, "because it was the shortest and quickest way," and he reminded me of our experience in Domfront. After all, Chartres was a main road junction. I argued that the risk of being caught in Chartres was too great, so we should change our strategy and make a left detour around the town. This we did, and wound up right smack at an airfield. No sooner did we realize that the road had led us to the edge of an airfield than we spotted a formation of heavy bombers with fighter escorts. The fact that they did not fly toward the airfield let us breathe easier. But not for long. When we saw them right in front of the sun, they suddenly turned in a ninety-degree angle, and came towards us.

Historians say that the German Luftwaffe (Air Force) had less than two hundred planes in France at the time of the invasion, and only about half of them were really operable. One reason for the feebleness of the Luftwaffe was surely the fact that several squadrons had been withdrawn from France to the Reich to combat the air superiority of the Allies there.

The bombers attacked out of the sun, a commonly practised method, because German AA (anti-aircraft) guns would then be forced to fire against the strong sunlight. Later I would see this stratagem being used frequently.

Although we were at the edge of the airfield and thought we were well protected by a little earth wall, when soil began flying all over us as the heavy bombs exploded I was luckier than Alfred. Not only was he covered by earth while lying on the ground, but also a heavy rock fell on his back, which would cause

Coltainville, 1986(above) and 1994

him great pain for weeks to come. When we got up — I had to help Alfred get out from under the pile of earth — we saw that the single light plane which the Germans had gotten into the air was going down in flames. [25]

I do not remember how we got to Coltainville. The sun was going down and there was a small château. The doors were unlocked but the place was deserted. The beds had mattresses and coverlets but no linen, which of course did not bother us in the least. Somebody must have lived there not long before, as oil paintings were still hanging on the walls, and we wondered how long it would be before somebody ransacked this beautiful place. We chewed on some dry bread, because that was all we had left, and then went to bed. This night in Coltainville passed without any particular events. Not knowing what the next day would bring, we slept the sleep of the innocent, in the truest sense of this word (from the Latin for unknowing). Our sleep was deep and long. It was mid-morning when, with empty stomachs, we left this pretty little château. [26]

What happened next took place near Ablis. I remember it well. We had walked along the main road again and passed some kind of a mill or factory, as well as a railroad crossing, when we saw a passenger car coming towards us. We got a real shock when we realized that its occupants were Secret Field Police. They passed us, and we heaved sighs of relief. I turned around, and suddenly became aware that they had stopped about one hundred and fifty meters behind us. There were three of them: the driver, another low-ranking Field Police soldier and a major. The two former were armed with submachine guns; the latter carried a pistol.

The first one, with an obviously loaded submachine gun, got out of the car. We shouted to him in German and waved our admission passes for the construction site. We wanted him to see that we had no sinister intentions. Next, the driver got out, also holding his firearm in a ready to shoot position. We started again with the fake explanation for our being there in France. Finally, the major, with his pistol drawn, approached us. Again we gave

Above - S.C.A.R. Ablis, silo. Below - old railway station at Paray-Douaville

our fabricated account. All seemed to go well as we answered the major's questions, until he asked why we had not reported to one of the control posts along the way, which we could not possibly have missed. We replied that there had not been any such post on our route. Now the major's voice got even sharper: "You intentionally avoided these posts!" Moreover, he left no doubt, he did not consider our construction site papers valid at all.

Not giving us credence in any way, he said with a low voice: "Something is fishy here — turn around and start walking!" Immediately it flashed through my mind, they would claim they shot us when we tried to flee. Alfred looked white as chalk, and I probably not much different. My knees were shaking. This is the end, I thought. The major commanded "Safety catch off!" —

What Alfred and I did not know, and were in the end fortunate enough to live to learn about, was:

a) As soon as the Allies had landed, the Germans enacted Martial Law. The desperate Field marshal Kesselring ordered the shooting on sight of any Allied agent, whether in uniform or not.

b) International teams had been parachuted secretly into France before the invasion started. Their purpose was to gather French anti-Nazi people who, together with the Maquis, were to carry out hit-and-run attacks against the Germans, particularly against installations of military importance. Under the code name of Jedburghs, or Jeds for short, they were part of OSS operations. OSS was the Office of Strategic Services, an American cloak-and-dagger organization. Some were dropped over France as early as May 1944, others over Brittany in the significant invasion month of June 1944.

Considering these two points, together with the fact that we had no really valid identification documents, one can easily understand that our survival chances were almost zero.

However, even the German Secret Field Police cannot kill somebody if fate — or whatever one may choose to call it — does not agree. You don't believe in miracles? I do now.

Let me continue:

At this moment we heard a car coming from the rear. Disregarding the orders from the major, I turned around and opened my arms, to stop this passenger car. Our only chance to have a witness. A lieutenant of the German Air Force got out and asked what was going on. I quickly explained that the major did not believe our passes, but I was sagacious enough not to make any accusations. I did not want to antagonize the major, but hoped to resolve our dilemma by giving the Secret Field Police the chance to change the situation without losing face.

As it turned out, the lieutenant had been with the Air Force Construction Command in Cherbourg, under whose direction rocket launching sites were built. He must have known that this was accomplished with slave labour given to them by the SS/RSHA, and guarded by armed members of the OT, but this was irrelevant at this point.

To this day, I am totally convinced that the man knew very well who we really were, but he merely confirmed that civilian workers from Germany, mostly foremen, worked on the construction sites, and that the passes we had were genuine and exactly the ones issued to persons authorized to enter these construction areas.

Furthermore, the passes proved that we worked there up to the invasion, because we had the stamp revalidating our admission licence for the month of June 1944. What the lieutenant did not say was, we could not have lost our papers at the beginning of the invasion during the bombing of our lodging while we worked on the construction site, because the invasion started in the night when nobody was working. Our cock-and-bull story was just not airtight.

With luck, nobody found this out. [27]

He asked us what our plans were, and we replied promptly that we intended to go to Paris to report back to our company. Fortunately, nobody ever inquired where this company's Paris branch office was. Although we knew the name of the German construction company which got the contract from the Air Force Construction Command and the people from the SS/RSHA, to my knowledge, they did not have a branch in Paris.

It is my presumption that the major was not keen on having an officer witness a doubtlessly unjustifiable killing, particularly since the latter had testified that our assertions were true. Without saying anything further, the major told the driver to start the car. The soldier backed towards the car, yet his submachine gun was constantly pointed at us. When the engine was running, the major moved back to the car in the same ridiculous fashion, then checked the inflation of all the tires. Finally, the last man of this gang backed to the car. As the car began to roll slowly, the last soldier jumped in, closed the door and they took off at high speed.

I imagine, the major of this patrol must have believed that this was some kind of trap set by Jedburghs and/or Maquis.

Seeing our great relief, the lieutenant asked: "Now where do you really want to go?" With straight faces we answered: "To Paris". "Look," said the officer, "I can take you to any point before reaching the city. However, there are controls on all the roads leading into Paris, like a ring around it, and, since I am not permitted to transport civilians and you do not have proper movement orders, I would be in very hot water myself if you were with me."

Thanking the lieutenant for being so open and helpful, we suggested getting out of his car at Etampes, about fifty kilometres south of Paris.

It was afternoon when we shook hands and said good-bye to the officer. He had even given us part of his rations, because we had not eaten anything for a long time. Despite the fact that we had neither money nor ration cards, nor indeed anything left we could exchange for food, we were in remarkably good spirits. We had just escaped from an unbelievably dangerous situation.

Somewhere in Etampes stood what was no more than a hut. A sign in German said: Air Force / Paymaster's Office. If you have just jumped from the gravedigger's shovel, you do not have too many scruples left. With all the "guts" we could muster, we entered and found a sergeant and a soldier apparently busy packing up. We explained to them that we were employed by the Air Force Construction Command in Cherbourg. Then we gave them our yarn about the lost papers, etc., that we had not received any regular pay — let alone separation pay — since the invasion and were without a sou.

Without flinching, the sergeant took a form, entered the numbers of our admission passes which showed the name, Air Force Construction Command Cherbourg, printed on the head of the form, asked how much separation and regular pay we usually got per week, took our word for it and paid us thousands of francs. He made sure, though, that on the form there was plenty of room in front of the figures showing the sum we got paid. I am convinced that after we left, they added a few extra figures and pocketed the money. But why should we have cared? Be that as it may, we now had something to start with, including some bags of saccharin, for possible bartering.

In Etrechy, we stayed overnight in a barn, and then moved on to Paris where we hoped to be able to disappear in the throngs. There was no further control post on the road we took although, this time, we had made plans to circumvent any road block should there have been one.

8. — Paris

There are several blank spots in my memory, I must admit. For instance, I remember walking over a Seine bridge and crossing Place de la Concorde with the sole coming off my right shoe, but cannot recall how I got it fixed. I am sure I did not run around for months with an unmended shoe, and the boots we had in our sacks when we left Valognes had been exchanged for food on our way through Normandy.

Even though a few of the details are not clear to me anymore, most of the main events are still deeply and clearly engraved on my mind.

Alfred and I turned left on Place de la Concord and went along the beautiful and impressive Avenue des Champs Elysées, seeing the famous Arc de Triomphe in the distance. Certain things, however, spoiled the otherwise lovely picture. German soldiers and SS in uniform sitting arrogantly in the outdoor cafés. Magnificent buildings lining the avenue, confiscated or at least occupied by the Germans, flying one type or another of ugly swastika flags. It was not only our personal aversion to anything demonstrating Nazi domination, but also that it just did not fit. It was an offensive disfigurement of Paris. Aside from passing through en route to Valognes, neither of us had ever visited Paris before. [28]

We rode on the Métro to several "arrondissements" to look for a place to stay, preferably an inconspicuous boarding house. There were a few in the St. Michel area. As soon as we inquired about the price of a room, we were asked for identification papers, issued by the local authorities. These, of course, we did not have. Finally, we came to a house where the landlady was prepared to let us stay, although only for three nights. The price was reasonable and she was tactful enough not to ask bothersome questions. She even gave us ersatz coffee in the morning and soup in the evening. How could we ask for more? It bought us time to explore the grounds.

During these few days, we were constantly hungry, because we did not have any ration cards and could not afford the excessive prices that were asked for food on the black market. A slice of bread here, a little bit of salad there, was all we could get.

As we stood on the platform of the Métro station Réaumur-Sébastopol on our third day in Paris, waiting for a connection across the Seine, we actually bumped into a friend from Saxony who had also been transported to France because of his Jewish descent. He had not been sent to a forced labour camp but was held in the Caserne Mortier. One can imagine our surprise at seeing him go through Paris without being escorted by a guard.

At first he seemed as astonished as we were, but he quickly

pulled himself together and suggested that we go to a little restaurant outside the Métro, perhaps have a beer, and discuss what was happening all around us. We told him about our escape, and that we did not have valid papers or ration tickets, or even a place to stay the next day. Then, we inquired about his situation and things in general.

What he told us was, he had no idea whatsoever why he had not been sent to a labour camp, but was instead kept in Paris to do office work. For months, he and others were not allowed to leave the Caserne Mortier. The food was terrible and scarce. Almost every day at the Caserne Mortier, which then should have been called more appropriately "Caserne Mortuaire", they were threatened with being sent to St. Cloud, where the SS Correction Camp was. But all this changed a few days after the invasion. They were treated more decently, got better food, and were even given a pass for a few hours to leave the barracks every now and then.

He strongly suggested that we report back to Caserne Mortier, because conditions in Paris meant that we would most likely not be able to get a hiding place or food anywhere, and would be in constant fear of being caught. German controls and French informers, planted by the Vichy Government, were all over, and he knew of cases where escapees had been caught and executed. If we returned to Caserne Mortier, he would make sure that we got identification papers. Then, if on one of our leaves into the city, we found a safe place, we could still choose to leave Caserne Mortier.

This sounded very good, but somehow too easy. We were thinking of all we had experienced. Not that we did not trust Fritz. We just did not expect the SS to suddenly change their policy, become kind people, and make our lives easy, when not so long ago they were sworn to the motto "destruction by labour". What about our escape from Valognes? Fritz said that, because of the invasion, there was total confusion in all the German administrative offices, be they military, OT or SS. Nobody knew where anyone from the labour camps was, and lines of communication to Normandy, or indeed the whole of western France for that matter, simply did not exist anymore. This, he said, was also the reason for the relaxation of conditions in Caserne Mortier. The SS simply did not know what was coming and had switched to a sort of holding policy, with some behavioural correctness.

That evening Alfred and I had a long discussion. The change at Caserne Mortier could be only temporary. When the time came, the SS would certainly not surrender us to the Allies. As soon as the Allied armies closed in on Paris, we would surely be evacuated, or even worse. Also, what would happen if Otf. Leutner or one of his armed OT guards showed up in Paris and identified us as escapees? On the other hand, it would be very much to our advantage to have better papers than the construction site passes. We could then move about with greater ease and prepare for another escape, putting distance between ourselves and Caserne Mortier. Another very important factor in our deliberations, of course, was food. In short, we could buy time.

So, the next day we reported back to Caserne Mortier. As Fritz had promised, he arranged for new "Ausweise" (identification papers), which would be recognized by the authorities. How he managed to have them drawn up without indicating our Jewish origin, and then have them signed by the SS-commander, remains a mystery to this day. He was not prepared to tell us. After three days, we got leave passes for a period of five hours.

During this time we were stopped and checked twice in the streets of Paris, once by military police, and once by Gestapo in civilian clothes. Both times we encountered no problems, thanks to our new documents. What if this had happened on the first three days in Paris, or if we had not followed Fritz' suggestion? Only then did we realize how dangerous Paris was, and that the throngs of the big city were no protection at all.

Through Fritz, we got the news about the attempt to kill Hitler on July 20th, 1944. We could not believe that it had failed. What now? The war could have ended right then. Unfortunately, there was no word about any progress by the Allied forces either and, because we were impatient, everything seemed to be stagnant. With the great armies locked in stalemate, SS/RSHA and Gestapo had time to restructure their dirty work. We certainly did not like this unsettled situation.

Knowing about the cut-off communication lines, Alfred and I were prepared to stake everything once more on one card. We went to the OT-Oberkommando West and asked for the officer in charge of civilian workers. Brazen-faced, we gave him our yarn, how we suffered during the invasion days, how hungry and exhausted we were, and that we would like to have three to four weeks to recuperate. The officer said that this would be too difficult because, not only had all military leave trains been cancelled, but also all non-military personnel were forbidden to leave France, except for the wounded, of course.

Strangely enough, the OT officer, whose rank I cannot recall, did not even ask us for identification cards. For some reason, he trusted us and what we had told him implicitly. He told us a sob-story about how difficult it had been for him with his responsibilities, etc., etc. We listened attentively and expressed our sympathy on the burden of his duties. Finally, he asked us to come back in a few days and he would see what he could do.

The greater the chance of the Allies gaining a permanent foothold on the continent, the tighter the controls by the Gestapo, SS and military in France became. After serious deliberation, Alfred and I decided to try to go back into the lion's den, to Germany. No matter how relaxed the situation was at Caserne Mortier for the time being, this would surely change in time and definitely to the disadvantage of the inmates. The confusion among the German occupation forces in France would not last forever. As soon as there was a consolidation of front lines, the chaos would end, and the SS would again act in their well-known fashion. Finding hiding places in Paris was as hopeless as anywhere else we had been. Because we lacked knowledge of the language, we could not pass as French, whereas in Germany we would be able to talk in our mother tongue without attracting attention.

Through Fritz, we had in our possession some cans of meat and a few pounds of artificial honey. We still had our saccharin and several thousand francs. When the guard was tied up in conversation, we passed through the barrack gate with our precious items. Going north on the Métro, we reached Le Marché aux Puces (Flea market), where we spent about an hour bartering our goods for a fine briefcase made of pig-skin and a pair of ladies silk stockings. Don't ask me why we chose these two items. I do not remember.

A few days later we went back to the OT officer and talked to him again, indicating that, if we were sent to Germany to recuperate, we would not need the briefcase anymore. And, by the way, we just happened to have a pair of new silk stockings with us. The situation was tense, because we could not have been more obvious about our intention to bribe. Instead of throwing us out of his office, the OT official picked up the telephone, talked to somebody about giving us a medical check-up, wrote down an address and the time we were to see Dr. X (I do not remember his name) the next day.

With the help of Fritz, we obtained passes for that day and were able to make it on time to the address given to us. Nobody could have been more surprised than we were when we arrived at a medical office for — — — the SS. I cannot deny that we were overtaken by extremely mixed feelings but, since we had gone that far, we decided to play our roles to the end. The doctor asked us to strip to the waist, examined us very superficially, and told us that we would qualify for a "transport" to Germany. Another phone call and we knew when we had to be at the Gare de l'Est.

Before returning to Caserne Mortier, we went back to the OT officer, thanked him for helping us to recuperate for a few weeks, and left our briefcase with the silk stockings in it on a visitors' chair in his office.

Fritz was absolutely flabbergasted on seeing our official movement orders. We could leave Caserne Mortier to catch the train the next morning with authentic papers. We felt relatively secure for the first time in many months.

The rest of this particular episode can be told in very few words. When we arrived at the train station, we were the only two civilians among uniformed men. Everyone, including us, received a parcel with travel rations consisting of food, a bottle of cognac and cigarettes. After we had passed through the control post, we were allowed to board the train. Who could describe our feelings? At least, for the time being, we had no worries about food or where to stay because we possessed papers with official SS stamps both from the Caserne Mortier and the SS medical doctor, which should come in handy back in Germany. Papers issued by the SS counted for more than those from any other government office.

The train had to stop frequently, because of air attacks and destroyed railway tracks. In air raids, we ran to whatever protective ditch or wall was nearby. In those days not many trains were running. The French railway-men were afraid to ride in frequently bombed areas but, nonetheless, they used their expertise to make their locomotives inoperable.

Be that as it may, I do not remember the final destination of this train, only that Alfred and I got off in Leipzig, Saxony. That was the last time I saw Alfred. After the war, I tried to find him, but without success.[29] We knew, it would be extremely difficult to find a hiding place for two and, therefore, had decided that we would each stand a better chance of finding a hideout alone. Anyone willing to risk sheltering an escapee would be significantly increasing such risk if he or she were to take in two people. From there on, each of us was on his own.

VII.
BACK IN GERMANY

In the First Months of 1945

It was just after dawn. A minute before, the trusty had pushed one slice of mouldy bread through the opening of the prison cell door. This was half the daily ration. He had also poured ersatz coffee into my small tin bowl. With some luck, the next portion could be expected in the evening. At noon, the standard meal was a bowl of cabbage soup: at least that was what they called it, but one could not detect cabbage, meat, or any other solids for that matter. Even salt was lacking. Yet, I looked forward to getting these warm liquids, because not only did they pacify my hungry stomach for a while, but they also warmed me up a bit. The prison cell was cold and humid and, also, the seaweed-filled mattress was cold and moist. This combination created an awful smell. Ersatz coffee and soup certainly did not help one to collect any strength, but their warming effect usually lasted for ten minutes or so.

For three days, I had been in what the Gestapo euphemistically called "protective custody." The transfer papers, which I did not see until the war was over, were a bit more precise: confinement.

After my escape from a slave-labour camp at the German built Atlantic Wall, which had been controlled by SS in occupied France, and, after a dangerous game of hide-and-seek with the SS, Gestapo and military police, I had found refuge back in Germany.

Good people had risked their lives hiding and feeding me. I had also met their daughter, with whom I had fallen madly in love. We had sat in an air-raid shelter while the whole neighbourhood was blasted away by aerial mines, so-called blockbusters; we had run away from falling bombs and treated wounded people together. On one occasion, when a big man was wriggling with pain as he lay wounded in the street, this delicate girl sat on him to prevent him from moving too much while I applied bandages. One day after a raid, she was looking for me. She came down a hill wearing around her head a smudgy, turban-like piece of white cloth which contrasted, together with her white teeth, exposed by a big radiant smile, with her nicely tanned face. She was also wearing terribly torn stockings, the result of being thrown down the cellar stairs in a day raid a few hours before. Even so, I still felt that she looked smashingly lovely.

With these people I had felt protected and safe, relieved, as the constant stress I had been under for years had subsided. One day, all of a sudden, this situation changed. In a bombing raid during which, fortunately, my life and the lives of my protectors had been spared, the hiding place was completely destroyed. All bombed-out civilians had to report to the authorities in order to receive new ration cards, clothing stamps, etc., and had to register their new addresses. My good protectors, namely the girl I was in love with and her parents, found shelter with their friends, but were unable to find a safe place for me. I know how desperate they felt. But having benefitted from their warmheartedness and unselfishness for so long, I decided that it was now up to me to find a solution, and to relieve them of their self-imposed and highly perilous burden.

Although deep down none of us believed it would work, I tried to convince them that I would find a hiding place somewhere in my native town. When we parted, their faces showed indescribable pain.

As soon as I reappeared in my home town, a "good German citizen", obedient to the Nazi authorities, informed the Gestapo of my presence. I was arrested on the street and brought handcuffed to the local police station, where even the highest ranking police officer had to play second fiddle to the lowest Gestapo agent. Some policemen tried to show their unshakable devotion and admiration for Führer and Reich, by hitting me hard and pushing my head against the edge of a wall until I fell to the floor. One of them, of stocky build and with a face like a bulldog, looked like a professional wrestler.

The local head of the Gestapo came later. Meanwhile, I had to stand in a corner and wait. Fortunately, my hands had not been cuffed behind my back, and I managed to secretly draw my wallet out of the inside pocket of my jacket, tear its contents into small pieces, chew, and finally swallow them. In this way, even the postcard-sized portrait of my protectors' daughter disappeared, also a piece of paper with the addresses of two or three underground organizations given to me by my brother-in-law-to-be, just in case I should be able to somehow reach his native Holland.

This happened not a second too soon, because the bull-faced policeman in charge of the shift, a man by the name of Schramm, returned and took me into another room where I stared into the face of the person who had vandalized my mother's apartment three years earlier. He had done this by pulling out drawers and turning them upside down, by tearing bed sheets and clothing apart, and by screaming and calling her all kinds of mean names. They had tormented her, and I was so upset that I had interfered physically. He could have arrested me then, but an internal power struggle with the chief burgomaster, who had done his utmost to at least moderate the Gestapo actions against us, had hindered him. Toward the last years of the war, however, the Gestapo clearly had the upper hand in such inside quarrels, and my arrest came just at the right time for Mr. Walter Arnold.[30] His cynical grin showed that my arrest pleased him very much. Then his face turned red, and he beat me brutally with the dog-whip which he always carried around. They emptied my pockets and the contents were checked.

When I was led into the cell at the police station, my relief at having been able to destroy incriminating and dangerous evidence which could have cost many lives, including those of my protectors, far outweighed the physical pain.

The next day had another special event in store for me. Gestapo agents drove me to their headquarters in the district city of Zwickau. I was led upstairs where the district Gestapo chief, Albert Agsten, was already waiting for me. We remembered each other well. With his ugly, pointed, bird-like head and beak-like nose, he, together with his pal, Dog-whip Arnold, had appeared at my mother's flat.

"Are you Jewish swine scenting spring air?" he sneered. This expression was meant to indicate that he recognized and dismissed as false my hopes that the Nazis would soon be gone. Then he slapped my face twice and had his helpers turn me around to face the wall. They knocked me in the back with some hard objects, probably pistol grips or rifle butts. Because most blows were directed against the kidney area, I soon fainted. I was brought to by a bucketful of cold water and their treatment started all over again. [31]

More carried than walking, I was taken to a waiting car which brought me to a prison admission office, where I collapsed again. When I recovered my senses, I heard the officials laughing gloatingly, because they believed I was faking the fainting spell. My belongings, including my wristwatch, were taken away, and I received an ID-tag with the number **212**. That was how I came to be in the solitary confinement cell No. 5 on the third floor of the Schloss Osterstein Prison.

The mattress in this cell rested on a wooden board. During the day it had to be folded up against the wall by means of chain links. Although prisoners were not permitted to sit or lie on the mattress, except at night, I did not care about the regulations at this time. I lay down anyway, because I was hurting all over, particularly my back. I still felt terribly sick and cold, even though I had wrapped a threadbare blanket around me.

Later, when I sat up and looked about, I found a tin plate, a tin bowl, and a spoon on the floor. In one corner was a toilet

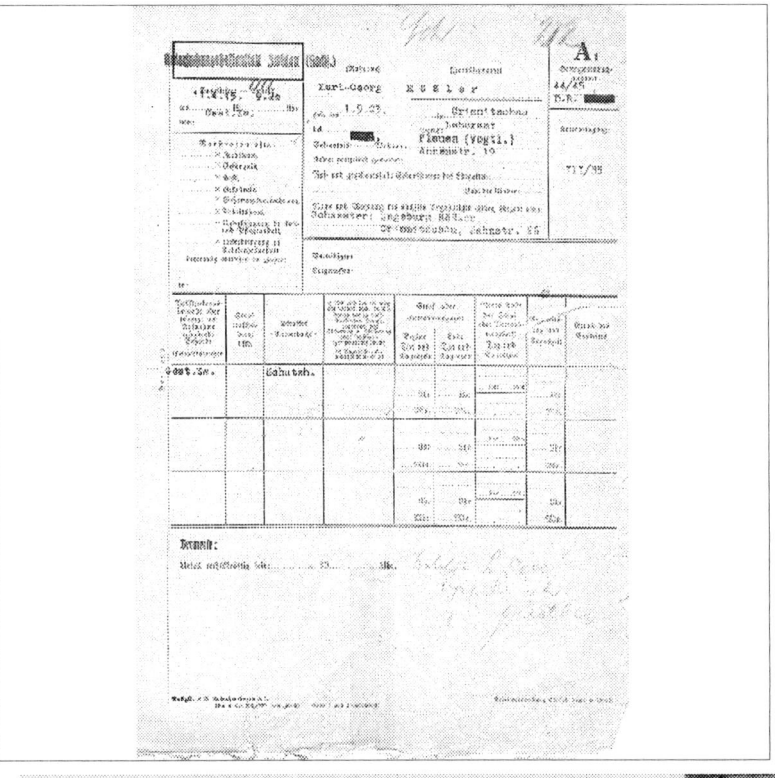

Above - Gestapo order for imprisonment ("protective custody").
Below - Schloss Osterstein Prison, Zwickau, Germany.

and, at the other end, about seven feet up, was a barred window with hinges at the lower edge and a snap mechanism with a rod attached to the top of the frame.

The cell seemed to be sound insulated. Although some muffled sounds came through the closed window, no noises could be heard from inside the prison. There was only the automatic flushing of a toilet every now and then, the knocking of the service hatch, or the clicking of the lid when the guard looked through the peephole.

Days passed with a lot of time for thinking. I tried to stay away from the unnerving guessing game of what the future might bring. The only safe assumption was that the Allies were drawing closer, but the non-military moves of the Nazis in these last months could not be fathomed by reason or logic. Consequently, I eliminated all speculative thoughts and adjusted myself to a waiting pattern of resignation.

In this manner, three days had gone by. The first important interruption of this stupor was the warm cabbage soup being passed through the hatch. Its distribution had been announced by the trusty banging a ladle on the cell doors at each building level. Cabbage soup seemed to be the Nazis standard fare for prisoners, not really deserving the name "food." We had been fed this liquid in the slave labour camp in France.

During the following night, a few bombs fell on the city. Although an alarm was sounded, the prisoners were not allowed into the air-raid shelter. One bomb damaged an end wall of the prison, and a few prisoners succeeded in making their get-away; later I found out that they were never recaptured. The hole caused by the bomb blast was quickly repaired, and prison life returned to normal.

One evening, I heard the first far away thumps which seemed to originate from heavy artillery, and I became enormously excited. The sky was clear and coloured by the red of the sunset. In spite of the cold, I opened the window and listened . . and listened . . . but there was no more shooting to be heard, neither that night nor the following day. My hopes vanished.

The next day, about three hours after the distribution of ersatz coffee, the key was turned and the cell door flung open. Orders were shouted, and all prisoners had to rush down to the ground floor. For reasons not known to any of us at the time, we had to line up in formation. There we stood for more than an hour, with SS and Gestapo coming and going, as if they were uncertain what to do next. Finally we were taken back to our cells. Why this exercise? A trusty who brought the evening bread portion and ersatz, as it was called for short, whispered to me that we had been scheduled for a "transport" to the KZ (concentration camp) Flossenbürg, but the "Amies" (Americans) had already crossed the railway lines to the south, making the planned transport impossible.

On this day at dusk one could hear frequent thumps, closer than I had heard earlier. Or was it only my wishful imagination? Maybe my expectations had deceived me, because there was no sound of guns on the following day. This, and the total silence in the cell, nearly drove me out of my mind. Only the meaningless clicks at the peephole, the pings at the hatch shutter three times a day, and my own movements when pacing the length of the cell interrupted the absence of sound.

There was hardly any standard routine in this prison. Prisoners were not walked in the yard or taken to a work place. Communication with others was virtually impossible. Because the prison used to be an old castle, signals by knocking against the thick walls could either not be heard or were not answered because the inmates were scared of being lured into a trap. More days passed without any indication that the Allies were advancing.

Suddenly, close to noon one day, distant machine-gun fire could be heard. This had an electrifying effect on my mind. It was as if a mental switch had been flipped. This instantly changed my mood from extreme depression to high hopes. Somehow, I sensed a certain tension building up in the prison, although I had no real proof of this. Was it telepathic, coming from all the minds of the prisoners focussing on one point: liberation?

The next day it felt like somebody had thrown a chilly blanket on me, choking all my hopes. There was no sound of gunfire of any kind. Had the Allies been repulsed? Did they retreat? Only temporarily? Although I had always fought it, I now started that mental game of guessing, which wears one down.

The cell felt colder than ever. The ersatz seemed to have lost its warming effect. Something very unpleasant and disquieting, yet indefinable, penetrated my mind. Then total pessimism settled in. With the Allies so close, would the SS do anything to us now, when the chance that they would be captured was so real? Would they be prepared to continue tormenting and killing people "five minutes to twelve?"

Since I had been in prison, tension had prevented me from getting much sleep. But now I was completely exhausted. The starvation diet, the cold, and the humidity had chewed away at my physical strength. The feeling of total isolation, and the uncertainty of what the future would hold in store for me, had drained my mind. All this had contributed to the fatigue which had finally caused me to fall asleep shortly after midnight. It could not have been more than a couple of hours later when I was wakened by the noise of heavy machine gun fire, and this continued without interruption until daybreak. When the trusty pushed the tin bowl filled with ersatz through the hatch, he whispered that the SS were planning something, but he did not know what.

It must have been eight or nine o'clock, when I started hearing muted banging of doors. There was no way of finding out what was going on. About half an hour later somebody pounded on my cell door. Shortly afterwards, the door was flung open, an SS man grabbed me and pushed me next to another prisoner in the corridor. Then two more men from the neighbouring cell were shoved out. Two SS guards with submachine guns escorted us into the cellar. We had to stand with faces against the wall. Sheer terror seized us, because we were standing in blood and saw blood splashed all over the wall.

There could be no doubt, prisoners had been shot right here and not too long ago . . . and we were undoubtedly next in line. A cold draft came from two broken cellar windows. As the guards took up shooting positions behind us, and a few steps up, about six or seven meters away, a bazooka was suddenly pushed from the outside through the bars of one of the windows and crashed down on the floor. It was clear in everyone's mind that the "Volkssturm" (last reserve units, consisting of old men and teenagers below the age of eighteen,) was trying to escape armed confrontation with the US forces and, therefore, was getting rid of their bazookas.

It would be quite impossible to describe the thoughts and feelings which flash through one's mind at a moment like this. Facing death and, also, knowing of the incredible closeness of the possibility of freedom, one is just a hair's breadth away from insanity. It would be ridiculous to shout any heroic last words, with just two murderers and three fellow prisoners present. Crazy as it may seem, though, such thoughts as this really did go through my mind.

The bazooka was of no help to us. Anyone making any attempt to grab it, would have been shot immediately. Even assuming for a moment that such a move was possible and that someone could have reached the weapon and pulled the trigger, the resulting explosion would, undoubtedly, have blown us all to pieces. Actually, it is somewhat surprising that the wretched thing did not explode on impact, considering the hard cellar floor.

However, the furore which followed the astonishing arrival of the bazooka proved in the end to be very helpful. At first we four prisoners were immersed in agony as we felt the sands of time running out on us, but then we heard a lot of shouting. Suddenly, one of the two executioners ran upstairs. He returned after a short while, which had, nevertheless, seemed like forever and, within a few minutes we were back in our cells on the third floor. We were still alive.

Shock is medically explained as being due to inadequate

volume in blood vessels, to inadequate functioning of the heart, to some other reasons, or to a combination of any of these factors. I firmly believe, my shock came as an after-effect of this horrible experience and could have been caused by a multitude of imaginable factors. I fell onto the mattress, unable to think clearly. My hands were shaking and my feet were both cold and perspiring. I was hardly able to breathe. In fact, I had the feeling as being somewhere far away from the sphere of reality.

How long this state of semi-consciousness lasted, I do not know. What I do remember is that, at one point, I climbed up onto the bed, i.e. onto the mattress attached to the wall in its folded-up position, and balanced myself on the snap catch bracket. With all the energy I had left, I pulled myself up to the window, just in time to see the SS-guards sneaking out of the prison gate in civilian clothes.

The window frame in my cell had two traverse pieces, meaning the window actually consisted of three little windows arranged side by side. If one could take the frame down somehow and turn it ninety degrees, it would make a fragile, but otherwise perfect, ladder. With the SS gone, I began to feel courageous. Because I was in a furious mood after I had overcome the shock, I pulled and jerked the shutter pole until the window support gave way and the hinges broke off. With my foot, I broke the glass and climbed up the bars, using the frame pieces as rungs. Because my weight was less than eighty-two pounds, the frame did not break. From this unique viewing stand I could see across the small prison forecourt to the prison gate, the street, and into the park entrance across the street.

Just a few minutes after converting the window frame to a makeshift ladder, I saw the first Jeeps driving very cautiously along the street. Most of them had a machine gun mounted on top, and a protecting steel shield in an upright position.

It should be noted that not every prisoner was in solitary confinement. Fellow inmates in other cells facing the street must also have smashed their glass windows, because a storm of joyous shouts came from the prison down to the passing US troops. Except for a quick glance in our direction, the soldiers obviously had to concentrate on possible snipers or traps while driving and occupying the city. Moreover, who could know we were not imprisoned criminals.

Soon the cheering subsided, probably because the prisoners were exhausted and had become hoarse from yelling. This I had actually anticipated and hoped for. When it was quiet for a moment, and the next Jeep turned up, I screamed repeatedly at the top of my voice: "We are political prisoners!"

Lo and behold, one Jeep turned towards the gate. When the lieutenant and a soldier knocked at the gate demanding entry, a non-SS prison guard came with a bundle of keys but hesitated to open up. At this point, a tremendous thunder of voices broke forth from all the inmates who had watched him. All the suppressed feelings of fear, rage, and desperation were transformed into swear words. This outburst caused the man to open the gate quickly. He was pushed aside by the soldier, and with the help of a trusty, eventually all the cell doors were opened.

Most prisoners ran out of their cells to greet and hug their liberators, and soon a laughing, yelling, singing and dancing crowd had gathered on the ground floor. But for some the liberation came too late. Not only were they emaciated to mere skin-and-bone, but also some had even been kept in total darkness since who-knows-when. Two of these inmates died instantly from shock when told that they were now free.

One prisoner in dark solitary confinement was a twelve-year old boy who had been admitted a few weeks before the liberation. His story will be told later. Another one was in reasonable physical shape, but suffered a nervous breakdown when the pressure of confinement was suddenly lifted. He embraced the lieutenant and his aid, broke down in tears, and could not stop crying.

When my cell was opened, I hugged the two Americans like everybody else did, but then went berserk. Maybe this was a blessing in disguise, a relief valve which prevented a mental breakdown or worse. With a narrow wooden plank in my hands,

I walked through the prison and smashed everything breakable I could find. In the kitchen, I spotted a huge paper bag with ground ersatz coffee and ripped it open. Windows, plates and cups — everything I could lay my hands on — I smashed to pieces.

Finally, I calmed down and began to coordinate my senses. I remembered that I had seen bread and margarine as I had gone through the kitchen, so I went back there and afterwards made my way to the prison gate holding a piece of bread with a thick layer of margarine on it. I wolfed it down. At the gate was the man who constantly cried, as well as the twelve-year old boy. They did not know where to go or what to do. All the other prisoners had apparently left already, and now the gate had been locked again.

In a room adjacent to the courtyard was the guard who had unlocked the gate for the Americans. I told him to open the gate for us immediately. At first he refused and tried in a typically German, bureaucratic way to explain that there was a curfew in effect, and nobody was permitted to be on the streets. He said it would be in our own best interest to stay inside. My fuse was rather short that day and, frankly, I could not have cared less about whether there was a curfew or not. My intention was only to get the hell out of the prison as quickly as possible, away from the place that had been abode of the damned, for all of us. In a loud and angry voice I demanded that he open up instantly, and called him all kinds of less than complimentary names. I even threatened to call the Americans and have him arrested for conspiracy with the SS and Gestapo. Though this was a bit absurd and really an empty threat, it worked.

Since everybody, including our two American rescuers, had already left, I felt it was my responsibility to look after the boy and the crying man. They were absolutely helpless. So the three of us went to find the US Army Headquarters. At this time, the sun was going down. Only single shots could be heard now and then. The ID-tag was still hanging on a string around my neck when we took our first steps into our newly found freedom.

Even though we must have looked like a bunch of animated scarecrows to the soldiers on guard in front of city hall, when I politely requested permission to see the Commanding Officer, we were admitted without any fuss to the hustling and bustling of the commander's "bee-hive". The troops had arrived only a few hours before, and yet cables had already been laid, and phones were installed. Staff people ran back and forth and dispatch runners came and left.

In charge of the local headquarters was a major of the US Army. In my limited school English, I was, nevertheless, able to explain to him where we had just come from, and to ask whether he could help us find accommodation for the night. His suggestion was very simple: "Go to a house or apartment, throw these @#$%^&*! Nazis out and sleep there." And that was it. He had, of course, other things on his mind. After all, he was not a quartermaster for three left-over prisoners. He still had a war to fight. This did not change the fact that it was getting late and dark, and we had to find a place to stay for the night. My trusting companions followed me like zombies. As much as it was clear to me that many high calibre Nazis would still live in the city, I also realized, the majority were merely followers, just nominal party members or even Nazi opponents. Just the same, the sad reality remains, most Germans watched silently what was going on, according to the principle of not attracting attention. In spite of my experience in the past, I never forgot: "Do not unto thy fellow man..." We certainly did not want to kick-up a row at the wrong place. People might not open their doors, because simply they were afraid.

There was only one strategy left: try asking for accommodation politely, but with no qualms about forcing our way into a home, if we should meet with any resistance or spiteful behaviour.

We came to a little house with closed window shutters at the street level, but with a gleam of light coming through gaps on the sides. I knocked at the door, which was immediately opened ... by a French POW. I explained our predicament, and we were asked to come in. To my surprise the whole apartment was occupied by French POWs, who had also been liberated that afternoon. I am not sure whether or not they had thrown out any @#$%^&*! Nazis. Anyway, they embraced us and immediately asked many questions. The sergeant, who must have been the senior man in this group, insisted that we first eat and drink before doing anything else — even talking. From the stove came the delicious smell of bean stew.

The ex-prisoner who had had a nervous breakdown was still crying and was unable to eat. For some reason, there were no beds around so our good hosts spread their coats and some blankets on the floor, on which my companion lay down. His crying soon changed into sobbing, and then, totally exhausted, he fell into a deep sleep.

The boy ate well. Although he spoke little, his eyes spoke for him. Big, wide open eyes, still filled with fright and fear. His father had been taken to a concentration camp for political reasons. His mother was in a forced labour camp. He and a brother had been sent to a Nazi reformatory, where they were kept under extremely harsh conditions. The boy decided to escape and first succeeded, but was then captured about one hundred and fifty kilometres away from the institution. Without hesitation, the Gestapo put this twelve-year old into dark, solitary confinement. Eventually he also slept, and the way he was lying on the coats indicated that he was now quite relaxed.

Then I started eating, and did so as if trying to catch up on all the food I had missed since 1939. Our French hosts had "confiscated" hard liquor from a German merchant who had concealed many such bottles in his cellar. How, after all those years on starvation rations, I was able to consume such large quantities of bean stew and hard liquor without becoming sick has been unexplainable to this day. The same goes for the bread with a thick layer of margarine which I had eaten at the prison gate. Knowing how other half-starved camp and prison inmates reacted to big portions of food, it really makes me wonder how my system managed to tolerate it all.

At the time, however, I did not give it any thought. We caroused, ate, sang and talked until the sky turned slowly to a golden-orange and the sun started rising. It was probably the excitement of our newly gained freedom which did not let us become tired. We had made toasts to life, health, happiness and luck. We had made toasts to girls, women and the more intimate things in life. At least every third toast was "Vive la France!", and I certainly had no reason to object to this.

One of the freed POW's came from Normandy and knew the place where I had been in the slave labour camp. This was one more reason to celebrate and drink a few toasts to "La Normandie". Although I never heard the melody and had always thought it was only a poem, I joined in an appropriate song: *"Quand tout renaît à l'ésperance...j'aime à revoir ma Normandie..."*, because these were words I knew. My mother had recited them repeatedly.

That morning, all of us drank r e a l coffee. Not that I would have asked our hosts any embarrassing questions, but it did seem to be quite a miracle that they could procure all these wonderful things within such a short time, things which were practically not available anymore, not even for Germans.

As it turned out, the Americans had given coffee, cigarettes and chocolate to the POW's, and this accounted for some of the goodies.

After a night's rest, my companion was quiet and reacted normally. He had obviously overcome his nervous condition. Because he lived in a suburb of the city, in the centre of which our prison was located, it was no problem for him to go home after curfew hours. Then two of our French friends and I took the boy to a Red Cross station. The people on duty were very friendly and promised to arrange for proper care for the youngster and a reunion with his family as soon as possible. The lad could hardly carry the food given to him by our French hosts.

It was time for me to say "Adieu et au revoir!" and "Je vous remercie de votre hospitalité excellente!". They insisted that I take some money from them to carry me over the next few days.

Hugs and handshakes followed, mixed with quite some emotion.

Walking into the hills, I felt that peace had finally come to me after these turbulent years. Breathing the fresh air, I realized that I needed to be alone for a while in contemplative solitude to collect myself, and to look at the simple but beautiful things in life, like spring flowers and trees with their new leaves.

A farmer, who was taking milk to the next town, offered me a ride on his horse-drawn carriage. I accepted thankfully. No, I was not in a rush. Now I could choose where to go and take my good time. "At this bank and shoal of time", I really and truly had the right to live the way I wished to live, commandeered by none other than my own will.

The day we were liberated from that prison was April 17th, 1945. [32]

Part Two

VIII.
— AFTER THE LIBERATION —

1. — Back to the Right to Live

Just as I was returning from the prison to my hometown, whom did I meet but one of those "gentlemen" who had pushed us from the sidewalk onto the road, during the Nazi era which had only ended a few days ago, spit out in front of us, called us bad names and believed he could not consider my mother a lady anymore, because she was Jewish? Such a character gazed at me from the other side of the road, took off his hat to greet me young lad, and shouted across, asking how I was doing. A sudden urge came up inside me to run over and paste him one. But, then I thought better of it and decided to ignore the man.

An altogether different matter was that I could not deny myself looking up the skunk who gave me away to the Gestapo. When F. saw me standing in front of his house door, his face lost all its colour and changed to a chalky greyish-white. Rather cynical, I inquired about his health and asked whether he ever imagined that one day I would pop up again. He started to whimper and swore he had never believed that they would beat me up, take me away and lock me up in a prison.

Then I asked him what he would think about being brought before the courts for denunciation, or "How about me smashing all the glass you hoarded during the war?" (He was a master glazier). Again, he moaned and implored me to be lenient. He said he would be willing to do all necessary work I wanted to have done and would not charge a penny.

He probably envisaged the sort of reparation on an individual basis that the German government had offered the surviving Jews and Israel in form of a pecuniary compensation for all psychologically and physically sustained wrongs and damages to bring the government's guilt balance back to zero.

I had not expected that the encounter with this "loyal citizen" would make me sick to my stomach. I turned around and left him with his fear. Why not let him stew for a while, I thought, just as we had to live every day in fear through all the Nazi years, only with the difference that he would never have to fear for his life.

My next speculation was how I could get to Plauen to the girl with whom I had hopelessly fallen in love.

There was no mail service in those days, neither were trains or busses running. Normally, one could not get permits by the occupation authorities to use a car except for taxis within city limits and for ambulances. There was also no gasoline available on the open market and, at that point the black market had not gone into full swing yet. It took a few more weeks for that. Without proper papers one was not even allowed to drive with a bicycle beyond certain district borders.

"First things first", I reasoned with myself, and went to the local US headquarters. A very friendly master-sergeant issued me a paper, saying that I had just been liberated from a Nazi prison, and "to-whom-it-may-concern" was asked to give me any help and assistance I might require.

Later that day, "Fortuna" smiled on me once again. Whom did I meet but a tavern owner, who was in the possession of two motorcycles and was also quite scared that at least one of his vehicles, if not both, would be confiscated? So he offered me the following deal: I should choose and take one of the motorbikes for safekeeping and use it as long as I would need it, as compensation for taking it in trust. He figured that no one would seize anything from me. Since I knew the man had no Nazi record, I did not mind helping him, and myself, at the same time. I chose the smaller but newer BMW machine and started to practice, because never before had I driven a motor vehicle.

It was not so easy to keep an eye on the road, although only inattentive pedestrians were in the streets at that time. I also had to operate the clutch, the gas and the brake, all of which, unfortunately, were installed at different ends of the vehicle. Despite all these obvious obstacles, I managed to drive along some streets until I suddenly came to a T-intersection. There I had to turn either left or right. This meant that, once more, I had to operate the clutch, shift into a lower gear, brake and reduce my speed. Directly in front of me was a very steep slope.

Because of being in a state of total confusion with the manipulation of the different handles and pedals, I turned the gas handle in the wrong direction. This accelerated the motorbike very vigorously. Dashing halfway up the grassy slope, I was just lucky enough to make a turn without sudden fall, buzzed back into the street with high speed and barely missed some people, bicycles and a handcart. At last I got my motorcycle slowly under control again. It was like a young horse and a rider getting to know each other. After this episode, I was as secure in driving as any longtime motorcyclist can possibly be.

The owner of a gasoline station, who had considered us to be normal human beings even during the Nazi-time, filled my tank from his "secret reserve."

With a dry crust of bread and a piece of cheese I proceeded to Plauen.

People had warned and advised me against taking the direct route, because this was leading through what was still combat area. It turned out, however, that the roundabout way I was using led through a combat zone as well. Although there did not seem to be any artillery, one could hear shooting from carbines and machine guns very close to the road. The Germans must have hidden in the fields because the roads were free, only controlled by US military.

After I had just taken a rest and eaten my bread and cheese, and was about ready to get on my way again, I was stopped by a US patrol-unit who refused to allow me to drive any further. Only after they had seen my paper from the US town headquarters did they let me pass, but pointed out that this was at my own risk. Apart from a few stray bullets from snipers whistling by, I had no dangerous experience on my way and finally found my charming girl with her parents, safe and sound. I had not been so sure about their well-being, because Plauen had experienced further serious bomb raids during the time I was in prison. The happiness in seeing each other again was both mutual and great because none of us had known whether or not the other one was still alive.

2. — The US Counter Intelligence Corps

At the time I lived in hiding in Plauen, i.e. after my escape from the prison camp in France, the heavy bombing of this city had caused severe casualties. Friedl and I tried to help the wounded in the streets. On such an occasion I met a British POW whom the Germans had released from the POW-camp for a few hours to help with clearance and other auxiliary work. After the war, upon my return to Plauen, I ran into this chap again, who told me that they had been transferred by the Americans into former German army barracks and expected to be repatriated shortly. "Why don't you come and visit me and my fellow countrymen at the barrack before we leave?" he said. This I promised.

The next day I found out that there were two former German military barracks at opposite ends of the city. Friedl, the girl I was so in love with, and I walked to a central place in town where the American military had set up a guard house. Naive as I was, I asked the soldier, whether he knew to which of the two barracks the former British POWs had been temporarily transferred, to be flown back home later to England. Very polite, the soldier replied that he was not familiar with the situation, but would ask someone immediately. Friedl and I waited outside the guard house, while he was on the phone. It did not take long until a jeep with two officers arrived. They asked us to get into the car, and we left without delay. I was pondering about how kind it was of these people to come, pick us up and drive us to the barracks, when we stopped in front of a villa. The tone in which we were requested to go into the house was, as far as friendliness was concerned, at least three notches below the one with which we had been asked to get into the car. As soon as we were inside the house, we were led into different rooms and were interrogated. We had wound up at the CIC, the American Counter Intelligence Corps.

As far as I was concerned, they were a bunch of bad eggs — unfriendly, gruff, not even showing a trace of politeness; they were not at all the type of liberators I had been so happy to see opening the gates of the Nazi prison.

First, I was asked to which unit I belonged. "Darned," I said, "I did not belong to any military unit, nor any political organization!" As though he had not heard it, the officer continued questioning me, "Where was your last position?" As in English, the German word for "position" could mean a military or, also, a professional position. I promptly named the company for which I had worked before I had been deported. Once more came the question: " and with *which unit*?"

This was going on and on for quite a while. Finally, I had to remove my jacket and shirt so this turkey could look under my arm.

Now I knew what it was all about. SS men had their blood type tattooed under their arms and the CIC believed that I was a member of the SS who had escaped in civilian clothes and, what is more, had asked suspicious questions.

At this point I really turned sour, called the guy names and started to curse and protest about the way a person, who only a short time ago escaped death, was being treated. This did not seem to make the least impression upon the CIC officer. With a grim face he put a revolver on his desk and said "I am giving you exactly five minutes to come out with the truth, because all you have been doing so far is lying!" With these words he left the room.

It was not difficult to sense the trick behind this behaviour which could have come right out of a Hollywood movie. There was positively no ammunition in the revolver, and, if I had only so much as touched the gun, they would have had an apparent proof that I was guilty in one way or another. After the indicated time, the officer returned and ordered me to get dressed again.

Meanwhile, what had happened was that they had also interrogated Friedl, although in a much more polite way, and had compared our statements. Having done this, they brought us back to the jeep and delivered us to the apartment of Friedl's parents, where they ordered us not to leave until further notice. We were placed under house arrest.

Inside, I was fuming and could have wished the worst on all American soldiers; on the other hand, I knew well that it was absolutely necessary to screen all suspicious persons regarding their past. It was mainly the personal insult when the CIC did not trust my word that I resented. I tossed these mixed feelings around for two days, wondering what would happen next.

The day I decided to stop "tossing," a jeep stopped in front of our house. The same two officers with whom we had been dealing requested to talk to Friedl's father. What could he say what we had not already told them? But, this discussion seemed to give them the certainty they had been searching for. Without a further word the two men walked out of the house. What was going on? Were we still or no longer under house arrest? When we peeked out of the window, we saw the two returning with four huge parcels. It turned out that these were filled with US food rations. The officers shook our hands as if they wanted to congratulate us on a very festive occasion and wished us all the best for our future. No house arrest anymore. For a while, we were speechless.

Yes, it became a sort of fiesta for us, because of all the foodstuff and the valuable rarities such as we had not seen in years — chocolate, real coffee, good cigarettes, etc.

A few days later, when we just happened to be at home, the

officers came back. I was worried when I saw them coming, because I was afraid that they had changed their minds and renewed their suspicions, no matter how unfounded. But no, they said that they were about to be transferred to another area and just wanted to say 'good bye'. Again, they placed several packages with food and rare things on the kitchen table. Only when the jeep with the officers waving had disappeared did we realize that we did not even know their names. It occurred to us, however, that, for security reasons, they would probably not have given us their real names anyway.

3. — Wedding Obstacles

Friedl and I had decided to marry. Since our intentions were absolutely final, there was no reason to postpone the wedding for any length of time. Therefore, I went to the Registrar's Office to make inquiries about the papers we had to show for the marriage application. The Registrar realized, of course, that many personal documents of people in the city had been destroyed in the bomb raids and did not take exception to the fact that I was not in possession of my birth certificate anymore. My identity card had always been considered an official document which he recognized as such. "However...," he said, "you have to bring proof of your Aryan descent."

For a moment, I was simply flabbergasted and had to gasp for breath. I drew a deep breath and cried out: "I feel the strong urge to pound the hell out of you for this insolence, this indescribable idiocy."

"Well," he protested, "I have the right to demand this paper of proof! We did not receive any written instruction to the contrary from our superior department yet!"

Because of bomb damage, only a few rooms of city hall were usable. Consequently, all work concerning the Registrar's duties had to be done in one single office. Although the war had ended a week or so ago, many people were still queuing up to report their dead. Maybe there were even a few who were there to have births registered. All of them turned around when I suddenly screamed like mad. But, the official still insisted on his bureaucratic convictions, and I left the Registrar's Office with the assurance that instructions would be handed down very soon.

What to do now? The highest authority in the city then was the US Military Administration. After I had determinedly worked my way through the ever access-refusing German receptionists and secretarial personnel, I saw a directory on the wall showing, among other offices, "Legal Branch: Lt. Aaronson." Immediately, I felt in good spirits as I was almost sure that this was the place where I would get help.

Lt. Aaronson was sitting at his desk in an office on the first floor and lifted his head with an inquiring expression on his face. I introduced myself and explained the reason for my exasperation. No sooner had I given my statement than Lt. Aaronson called the Military Police on the telephone and ordered them to bring over the Registrar and the Chief Burgomaster. Within fifteen minutes the official and the Chief Burgomaster, escorted by Military Police, marched through the door.

I had been so furious about the intended, or foolishly unintentional, impudence of this Nazi official, that one can surely imagine with what kind of satisfaction I saw the startled look on his face when he entered.

Although Lt. Aaronson spoke perfect German, he summoned an interpreter through whom he interrogated the two administration officials. When the Registrar repeated his standard excuse, that he never received any order to change former regulations, one could see that blood was shooting into Lt. Aaronson's head and, although calm on the outside, he asked with a rather loud voice whether the official realized the war had ended and the Nazis had lost. From the Registrar came a fainthearted "Yes". Then the lieutenant continued, asking if the man had seen the posters, which were displayed throughout the city, proclaiming that all laws promulgated after 1933, particularly those with political and racist content, were declared null and void. Obviously, the stupid official felt cornered but maintained stubbornly that he had not seen any such posters.

Since everything has its limits, Lt. Aaronson was obviously not going to pursue this interrogation any further. He only mentioned in passing that the man must be blind or walking through the streets with closed eyes.

The lieutenant then told the Registrar that he would be given ample time to think about what he had done, in fact two weeks. With a motion of his hand, he ordered the Military Police to escort the man away to prison. The Chief Burgomaster, who was formally the Registrar's superior, was released with a warning. He was told to call the City Hall employees together and duly inform them about the new military laws already made public through the posters.

I expressed my sincere thanks to the lieutenant, but he shrugged his shoulders and replied that it was only logical that drastic measures had to be taken. Finally, he wished me all the very best for the wedding, whenever it would happen.

The next day saw me once more at the Registrar's Office. This time I gave my question about necessary papers for the marriage a somewhat malicious twist, touching on the "Aryan question". The new public servant did not request "proof of Aryan descent." When he asked when we intended to marry, I said "in four days." The official declared emphatically that the Law of the Publication of the Banns (for three-weeks), had already been in force before 1933. As in most countries, an official notice had to be posted so that persons who wished to enter a protest against a planned marriage could make their complaint known.

This did not suit me at all. I became recalcitrant and maintained that we had to wait long enough because of the bloody Nazis, and that I was not prepared to accept the three-week waiting time involved in the posting of the notice. Even if the Law existed before 1933, I could not have cared less. At this point, the new Registrar realized that I was the enraged prospective groom who had caused his colleague's detention. He did not hesitate for a minute. He took me to his superior who was in the process of scraping the swastika on the Nazi eagle emblem from the official city seal. As his hands were all blue, he was embarrassed to receive somebody. Nevertheless, the head official did some quick thinking and immediately gave his permission for the requested short-notice marriage.

In Germany, only marriages registered with the secular authorities are valid. The bride and groom decide if this will be followed by a religious ceremony. Only the former is officially recognized, however. This is an old law and not a product of Nazi legislation.

We were requested to appear at the city hall at nine o'clock in the morning. Since the city was completely devastated and it had not been possible to clear the streets up to that day, we had to find our way over and between ruins to the appointed location. (Over seventy percent of Plauen had been destroyed.) Friedl's father and Dr. Anton K. came as witnesses. The latter was a good friend of ours who had languished in prison during the last years of the Nazi terror regime because of a fabricated charge. Perhaps, prison had been a blessing in disguise, as, otherwise, they would have deported him to a concentration camp and killed him there because of his Jewish origin.

While, as a rule, it is the bride and groom who are nervous on such a day, in our case, it was the Head Registrar (not the one who got himself into prison, but the "seal-scraper"). It seemed that it was difficult for him to revise his usual Nazi-version speech about Führer, Reich, Fatherland, race, German blood and soil, and produce a normal address. Whatever, the man was stuttering and made frequent mistakes in his speech. When the witnesses were supposed to put the rings on our fingers, he addressed Friedl's father as Dr. K., and vice versa. That was when Friedl and I had an inappropriate fit of laughter at a ceremony which is supposed to be very solemn.

Friedl's mother was lucky to have procured a few pounds of shortening, after a nearby German military depot had been disbanded. For our wedding "festivities," she baked doughnuts. Unfortunately, there was not enough food available to prepare a real meal with meat and vegetables — not even for the five of us, to say nothing about wine or any other alcoholic beverages.

Despite this terrible shortage of provisions, we all had a jolly good time. We had survived the Nazi era and I had not only found my great love again but also could now look forward to a lifetime with her.

IX.
A MOTHER COMES HOME

To grasp how unreal the following was, one has to consider this situation:

Friedl's parents and we had been assigned a small flat as a temporary residence, although nobody knew just how "temporary" it would be.

The city of Plauen was too big for one person to know all the others, as it is in small towns. In the first weeks after the war, it was hardly possible to find any family who had moved, because of the high percentage of destroyed houses and, consequently, the many changes of addresses. Almost all the police registration offices, with their address records, had been bombed to pieces.

I have experienced too many situations to deny the reality of miracles merely because human mind is unable to explain them.

For example, a demobilized German soldier had walked from Czechoslovakia to Germany. On the way he received from who-knows-who a piece of paper addressed to me in Plauen without street address, although even this would not have helped anymore. The message was from my mother, saying she had survived the concentration camp and was hoping we, her children, were still living, too. She would like to be taken home.

(At this time in Czechoslovakia there also was neither mail service nor transportation.)

This man came into Plauen which once had about 123,000 inhabitants and was almost totally in ruins in May 1945. Only at the city boundaries did people still live in undamaged houses. In the centre, "cave dwellers" occupied makeshift quarters, mostly in cellars.

This man delivered the message to my parents-in-law while I was out, without explaining how he found us within this vast stone labyrinth, where people lived nearly in anonymity. It is inconceivable that he was actually able to bring us the paper with the message from my mother. My parents-in-law were so stunned by the fact that a message from my mother reached us, that they totally forgot to ask the soldier how he found us.

The whole matter becomes even more mysterious, if one learns what had happened before.

Although liberated by the Soviets, the inmates of Theresienstadt were not allowed to leave the camp, because of quarantine regulations at that time. My mother gave the message for me to a demobilized German soldier who happened to pass by the camp, but who marched *south* to Austria. He in turn met another soldier who made his way north towards Saxony, and the latter was the one who came into Plauen after prevailing through many obstacles in the already described post-war chaos.

Czechoslovakia had ceased to be the German "Protektorat" and was once more a sovereign state, although at this particular period the autonomy was for a time more internal than external. A demarcation line running from north to south temporarily separated the country into two military occupation zones, with the Soviets in the eastern part and the USA in the west.

No information about this situation was available to the average person living in Germany, because radio stations had not started to operate and newspapers were not being published at that point. Moreover, I really did not want to ponder about political matters then, but had one much simpler thought on my mind: just to get my mother out of the KZ, cost what it may!

Next, I turned to Lt. Aaronson of the Military Government. He was most willing to help me to the best of his abilities. But, as ill luck would have it, nobody in this military government branch had the authority to issue passes beyond the German borders, e.g. into the Czechoslovak Republic (CSR), to say nothing about permits for a person with a vehicle. In the end, and thanks to him, I had a full tank of gasoline and at least a pass in my hands, permitting me to drive as far as the border.

I did not consider that the motorcycle had neither a pillion seat nor foot rests for a pillion-rider, quite apart from the fact that there was absolutely no possibility to buy such equipment in those days. At least the bike had a carrier on which one could strap a blanket.

With some provisions prepared by a frightened Friedl, I left shortly after daybreak.

It was a mild, sunny day with merely some local traffic on the streets. In the first hour or so, there were no road controls and I drove without stopping the fifty-five kilometres to the German/Czechoslovak border. There was some feeling of relief when, from a distance, I saw soldiers in American uniforms. Even as I came closer, none of them lifted their carbines. This certainly had a reassuring effect on me. One had to keep in mind that the borders were actually closed and no traffic whatsoever was going either way. Normally, one could not even dream of going into the CSR from Germany, even less on a vehicle with a German license plate.

To appear nonchalant, with a casual motion I pulled my pass out of my pocket and said I was in a rush. "Okay," they said, and I was motioned to continue. In no time I had reached Czech territory. My joy did not last very long, because I encountered another military patrol. In contrast to the border guards, they inspected my pass very thoroughly and declared, which I already well knew, that this permit had no validity in that area. "This is exactly why I am on my way to the US Military Government in Franzensbad!", I countered. Franzensbad (Frantiskovy Lázne) was the next town. They let me go, but not without admonition to take the shortest way to the US administration authorities. At this point, I deemed it advisable to do so and seek a pass for the region through which I intended to drive.

The officer in charge of the Allied Expeditionary Force in Franzensbad was Major J.E. Margolis, 1st US Infantry Division. At first, he was somewhat surprised to see somebody without any valid travel papers arrive on a motorbike with a German license plate. Also, it was my impression that he was suspicious about my story about my mother's message and my intention to get her from the Theresienstadt (Terezín) Concentration Camp. Eventually, he issued me a pass, which was good up to the demarcation line. He also had my tank filled up, however, only with the express stipulation that I promised to drop in with my mother on our way back. I assured him that I would do so indeed, thanked him profusely, and left.

I arrived at the demarcation line, the town of Loket (Elbogen), without any complications, but was then overcome by a feeling of uncertainty. During the past weeks, Germans had been put in mass camps and were later expelled from the CSR. It was quite understandable that the Czechs did not have any great sympathies for the Germans, after all the years of oppression and persecution by a German government. And here I appear on the scene, although myself persecuted, nevertheless, a German, on a German motorcycle, with a German license number, requesting a permit to travel right across the CSR.

To my great surprise, I met with a very friendly Czech official who also spoke German and Russian. After very little waiting, he issued a Propustka (in Russian: Propusska) in two languages which said there were no objections against the above-mentioned person (my humble self) going to Terezín. The date: May 30th, 1945.

Full of joy and gratitude that everything had gone so smoothly, I whizzed off in the direction of Teplice (Teplitz-Schönau), remembering well, that this was the town after which my Polish relatives (Toeplitz/Teplitz) were named (or named themselves), at the time in 1787 when the Emperor Joseph II of Austria required all Jews to take family names. Czechoslovakia was then part of Austria.

Amazed eyes followed my license plate, wherever I drove.

Permit to pass through Czech territory, 1945.

As I entered Teplice, a sudden hissing sound reduced my joy greatly. The air had escaped from the rear tire, causing a serious dilemma. Not only were repair parts rarities but almost unobtainable. Over and above this, I did not have any Czech money, nor did I speak the language.

After some hesitation, I decided to wait until a person with a friendly face came along, and doing so, I accosted a man in German. He not only looked pleasant but replied to me very kindly in German and walked me to a repair shop, while I pushed the motorbike. He asked the owner to help me with my blowout and said good-bye.

Not wishing to prolong this tale, suffice to say that, despite all material being scarce, the owner of the station repaired my tire perfectly and refused to take even a penny from me, although German money in those days still had a market value in the CSR. He wished me "good luck" and a safe return home.

There was much Soviet military in the area but, fortunately, I did not meet any troublesome controls. In the case of such an event, I would not have even been able to make myself understood. Since Czech is a Slavic language, Czechs, so I learned, always understand some Russian, and vice versa.

It was already twilight at the time I arrived at the turnpike of the liberated concentration camp, Theresienstadt. All my limbs ached, and I felt stiff from the long drive. Whether the guards were Soviets or Czech police, I cannot remember anymore. Whoever they were, they did not want me to enter the camp. Quarantine!

A spotted typhus epidemic had been detected in April 1945 and had reached its peak in May. On May 14th, the Soviet commander imposed a quarantine which was somewhat relaxed two days before my arrival. Nevertheless, at the end of a long discussion with the guards, I was warned that once I entered the camp I would not be permitted to leave it for quite a while. I insisted going into the camp and felt that one would have to take an 'act-and-see' attitude.

I did not have the faintest notion where my mother's quarter was. Also, I totally lacked orientation. Not only had it become dark by then, but also, this time, I had entered the camp at a different gate than when I had gone in illegally, trying to see my grandmother in 1942. Somebody told me I should go to the "Evidenz" and ask there about my mother's accommodation. The word "Evidenz" or "Belagsevidenz für Ubikationen" stood for a record office for (inmate) quarters. (Both words, then unknown to me, originate from the old Austrian administrative language.) When I finally found this office — Luckily they were still open!— I was informed that, according to their records, my mother was in the Home for the Blind.

Nobody can envisage my shock! Now I was sure that my mother had kept me in the dark about her condition when she wrote the message and I started to perspire and to tremble inwardly.

Making my way through the darkness, I finally came to the Home for the Blind. On the stairs at the first floor level, I met a woman who said immediately: "You must be the son of Mrs. Roessler!" I confirmed this and could not spit out words fast enough inquiring about my mother's condition. "Not to worry," the woman replied, "your mother lost weight, of course, like we all have since we arrived here, but, otherwise, thank God, she is well and not blind. All buildings in the concentration camp have been crammed with people right up to the roofs. The lofts even have bunkbeds and that is where your mother lives with many others. Let me walk ahead of you so that I can break your arrival to your mother gently, otherwise, she might get a shock." I agreed and followed her.

When the woman reached the attic, she yelled at the top of her voice, "Mrs. Roessler!" From where I was standing, I saw my mother lifting her head from the upper bed. She had already turned in. "Your son is here!!!" This had been the 'gentle' preparation.

With one leap my mother came down from her "deuxième étage bed" and ran to the stairs where we embraced each other. Tears were flowing not only from both of us, but also from the people who had rushed to the scene to see the unbelievable. The unbelievable was a person who had forced himself into the camp. One must not forget that many inmates had suffered in the camp for three years or longer. They had been totally separated from the outside world, not knowing anything that had been or was going on. I was the first civilian from the "free world" who came into this building, like a visitor from another planet.

As a rule, each camp inmate had just one pillow and one blanket. But they came from all sides to prepare a comfortable night's lodging for me. In the end, there was not much sleep that night for anybody in the loft. Everybody wanted to hear; everybody had questions, so almost all people living in the Home for the Blind were sitting and standing around me. It must have looked like an enormous pow-wow with just the campfire missing.

It was shortly before daybreak, when we lay down to catch a few hours sleep, but already the early morning was being used for strategic planning. Following the principle 'Better to go to the boss, than talking to his clerk!', I left for the Soviet commander's office right after my frugal breakfast.

Again and again, I tried to get access to the camp commander's building, but the Soviet guard constantly refused me entry. Realizing that I would not succeed in changing the sentinel's mind, I walked to the side of the headquarters and just happened to see a detachment of soldiers march in single file towards the rear entrance. 'Now or never', I thought and although dressed in civilian clothes, I rushed to the end of the column. Walking behind this group I entered, first the back yard and then the headquarters.

Nowhere was an officer in sight. My experience had made me persistent and I walked up the wide staircase to try my luck on the upper floor. Because it was so quiet, all rooms seemed to be empty. In one office I saw a female officer behind a desk. For reasons difficult to grasp, she did not appear to be surprised that somebody from the camp just walked into her office unannounced. Kind fate had it that she even spoke German. I believe that never before did I say so many words in such short a time

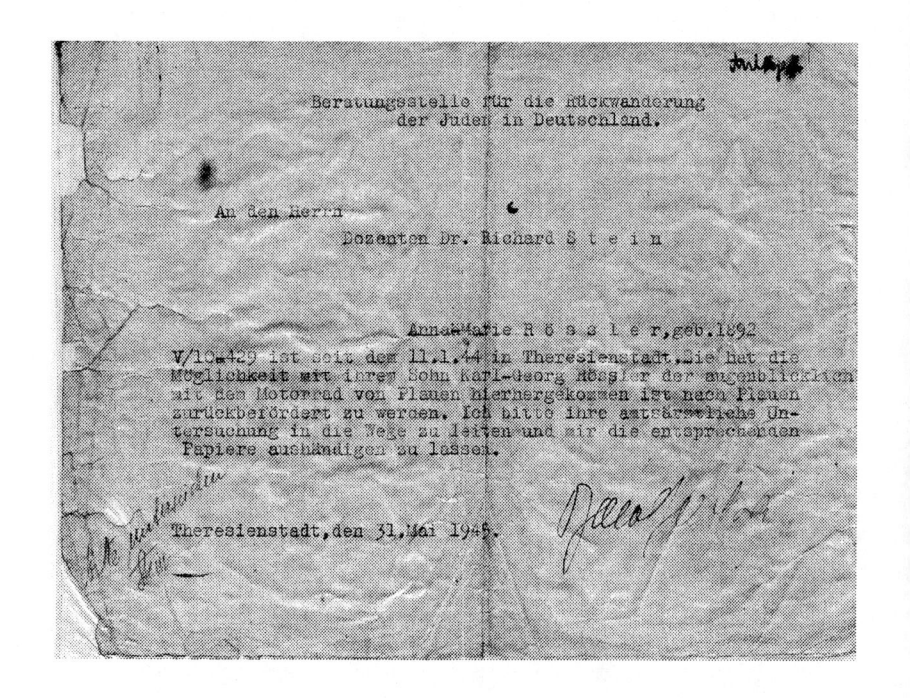

Beratungsstelle für die Rückwanderung
der Juden in Deutschland.

An den Herrn

Dozenten Dr. Richard S t e i n

Anna-Marie R ö s s l e r, geb.1892
V/10.429 ist seit dem 11.1.44 in Theresienstadt. Sie hat die
Möglichkeit mit ihrem Sohn Karl-Georg Hössler der augenblicklich
mit dem Motorrad von Plauen hierhergekommen ist nach Plauen
zurückbefördert zu werden. Ich bitte ihre amtsärztliche Un-
tersuchung in die Wege zu leiten und mir die entsprechenden
Papiere aushändigen zu lassen.

Theresienstadt, den 31.Mai 1945.

Medical authorization for author's mother to leave the liberated Theresienstadt (Terezín) concentration camp.

to explain my wishes. I implored her to help me to get an exit permit for my mother and myself.

"For which day?" she asked me. "For tomorrow morning, please," I replied with some hesitation, sensing the improbable.

She explained that this would not be easy to arrange but she would try. I should see her in her office around five o'clock that afternoon. To be sure that the guard would let me in, I asked her for an entry pass. With this paper in my hand, I walked out of the front door and gave the guard, who had not allowed me to enter, a dirty look.

Meanwhile, my mother had gone to the "Beratungsstelle für die Rückwanderung der Juden in Deutschland" (Information Centre for the Return of Jews to Germany). They made a formal request *in writing*. (Bureaucracy is always a priority!) Dr. Richard Stein, of the nearby camp's medical department, received this formal request to issue a certificate of non-objection for leaving Terezín. Before such an authorization could be issued, several offices in the camp had to certify that there had not been any spotted typhus cases in the Home for the Blind for three to four weeks. Then, dear Mom had to undergo a thorough medical examination, but, finally, she received the important document, a clean bill of health.

As one can imagine, I was very anxious with anticipation when I showed up at the Soviet commander's headquarters at five o'clock on the dot. The female Soviet major was in her office and accompanied me to the Commandant, who asked me, through her, a few questions in a short military manner and requested to see the certificate from the medical department. He then signed the exit permit without any red tape, shook hands with me, and wished us a safe return home and lots of luck.

I was surprised about his warm wishes, because he had struck me as a bearish, rough-and-tough fellow, an impression which was reinforced by the sound of his deep voice. One would not have expected him to say anything friendly to a stranger. However, I must admit that the Russian language as such seems to be crude, brusque, almost rude to the ear of a Central European.

Listening to Russians talk, I always had the feeling that because they spoke with loud voices to each other, they were arguing. In reality, it was regular conversation.

I cannot remember the eyes of the Commandant, but well recall the warm and soft eyes of the female major which contrasted with the harsh accent of her German. Back in her office, I assured her of my most sincere gratitude and asked her for her home address, which she gave me after some hesitation. Whether it was the real one or not, I should never find out, as I never received a reply to a letter of thanks which I wrote to her a few months later. Although I lost the address, I remember that she, supposedly, lived in Moscow. It must also be remembered that the Cold War with all its restrictions on Sovjet citizens followed.

That evening there was a big discussion going on in the Home for the Blind. Everybody gave good advice as to what we should do, how we should drive, et cetera. One thing was a sure fact, that, without foot rests and pillion seat, the whole trip would be an extremely shaky operation, particularly on this small motorcycle. It was impossible to take such a voluminous piece of baggage as my mother's bedroll with us. We promised to do our utmost to organize a bus immediately upon our return and to have the survivors from Plauen repatriated. The Plauen inmates assured us, they would reciprocate by bringing my mother's blanket and pillow on the bus. We kept our promise; the good camp companions, unfortunately, did not. In this way, my mother finally lost her scanty, very last and only possessions not confiscated by the Nazis.

On the morning of July 1st, 1945, I drove our loaded transportation vehicle in a sort of wavering fashion through the turnpike which had been opened after we had presented our passes. The guards' faces expressed utter surprise. For one, I am sure, because we were permitted to leave Theresienstadt in spite of the quarantine and, on the other hand, because of the strange way two persons drove on a motorbike. My mother had a little rucksack on her back and held a bag between us. I had to strap my rucksack in front of me. Frankly, I was worried about her, but she said: "Drive on, no matter how, just let us get out of this camp!"

Sometimes crazy images enter one's mind at unusual moments. When we wobbled the first hundred meters along, leaving the camp behind us, I thought of aircraft pilots coming back from a successful mission, waggling their wings.

At first, the desperate efforts to keep the vehicle-baggage-person complex in balance was like two circus artists trying out a new act on a horse that was not used to such tricks. Although told by me to do so, my mother did not want to cling to me, in order not to interfere with my driving. However, viewing things from another angle, she had no hold on footrests and was forced to keep her feet from getting into the fast rotating spokes. It must have been quite a sight! I suppose, as one can get used to the unrhythmical pace of a mule, my mother somehow managed not to fall from the carrier of the motorcycle, although she was without any support whatsoever.

Everything went well, until we reached Teplice (Teplitz-Schönau). There, we were lucky not to fall when the motorbike suddenly bucked. We had to put our feet quickly on the ground. This time the front tire was punctured. Once more — miracle of miracles — I succeeded in getting a repair shop to help us, and, shortly after, we were on our way again.

— Stop! Demarcation Line! —

During the last two days the Soviets had erected a heavy turnpike which blocked the entire width of the road. We stopped and showed our passes, but the Soviet officers with grim features did not want to let us through, although the passes were made out in Theresienstadt and that in Russian. They spoke neither German nor English but only muttered something in Russian and shook their heads.

For the first time I came across an example of what has

been demonstrated in politics again and again: In most cases one can only achieve one's purpose with the Soviets by acting relatively cold, unpolished, even crude and "intensely shirt-sleeved". Although I certainly could not deal from a position of strength, particularly since I could not even speak their language, I started to scold in a loud voice and with an angry grimace, constantly pointing to our pass. This drew the attention of the American officers, approximately ten meters away, on the other side of the Demarcation Line. My behaviour did not make the Russians friendlier, but the clamorous situation in the presence of the "others" may have been somewhat embarrassing for them. At any rate, the one Russian officer made a grumpy motion with his head toward a soldier who in turn slowly pulled up the turnpike and let us pass.

Though my mother assured me she was all right on her seat, it was clear to me that she had to be most uncomfortable all the time, and, by now, must have felt every single bone in her body. I stopped in Chomutov (Komotau) in front of the US Military Government branch and entered the office where the daily affairs of the population were dealt with. A bull of a sergeant was sitting behind a desk, with an unfriendly face and a rudeness which by far exceeded the Russians we had just met. With the shortest words he could find he barked at me, saying that he would not give us a pass through the US-occupied region of the CSR and there was no accommodation at this locality "for people like us" (whatever he meant by that). Furthermore, we could not get anything to eat in town, and ration tickets would only be distributed again in a month.

It was not really "what" he said that rubbed me the wrong way, it was "how" he said it. There did not seem to be a good reason for trying to argue with this bully. Therefore I turned around, left the building with a 'what-the-hell' feeling, and told my mother that we would drive on even without having proper papers. She definitely felt already better after having stretched her legs a bit and had no objections concerning my decision. The prospects to have a meal soon were rather poor indeed.

Only once were we stopped by Czechs who let us go without delay when we showed them the Soviet-approved exit permit from Theresienstadt.

Then we arrived in Frantiskovy Lázne (Franzensbad.)

I remember the time we spent at the US Military Government there as if it had been yesterday.

At the moment we entered the front office there was no one around, but somebody must have heard us, nonetheless, because a member of the Women's Army Corps came and asked us whether she could be of any help. I explained, I had given Major Margolis my solemn word to drop in with my mother on our way back, "... and here we are!" The secretary left the room and returned shortly after with the major who embraced my mother so affectionately, as if he were her own son. He cheerfully exclaimed: "Welcome, Mom! It is so good to see you are well!" Immediately, he asked us to sit down and then whispered something to his secretary. While we talked about Theresienstadt and how we got to Franzensbad, the Army Corps helper served excellent coffee and sandwiches which we did not allow to get stale, as one can imagine. When she also brought three large parcels containing food rations and other goodies, our eyes opened wider and wider.

As much as we appreciated all these gifts, we were unable to get even half of them into our small baggage containers. Only very few of these rarities could we stuff into our rucksacks, no matter how much Major Margolis tried to talk us into taking more of them. The same happened with gasoline. After my tank was filled, there was no possibility to take more, although full canisters would have been also at my disposal. Too bad!

When Major Margolis asked if there was anything else he could do for us, I asked him for a pass which would permit us, if necessary, to drive even during curfew hours. My calculation was that we would arrive in Plauen before curfew hours started, but I liked the idea of a built-in safety factor. One could foresee delays caused by, say, another blow-out. There was also the possibility of running into delaying control checks, etc.

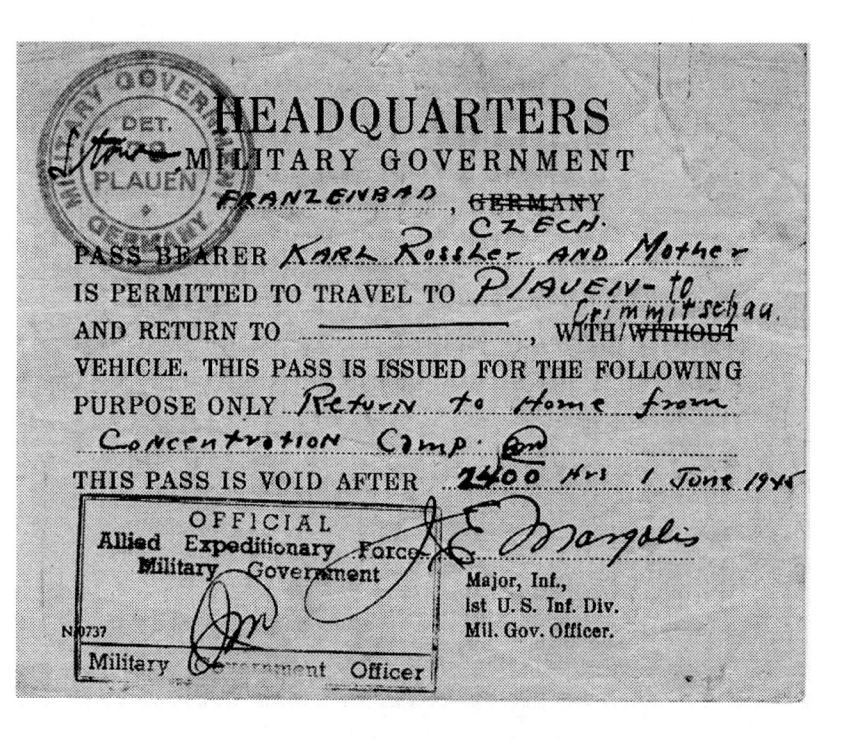

Allied (US) travel permit to return from
Theresienstadt (Terezín) concentration camp.

We received the following document from the major:
"HEADQUARTERS, MILITARY GOVERNMENT, Franzensbad, Czechoslovakia.— Pass bearer K.G.Roessler and mother are permitted to travel to Plauen, with vehicle. This pass is issued for the following purpose only: Return to home from concentration camp. This pass is void after 24:00 hrs. — 1 June 1945.
Signed: J.E.Margolis, Major, Inf., 1st U.S. Inf. Div., Mil.Gov.Officer. "Stamp: "OFFICIAL. Allied Expeditionary Force, Military Government, Military Government Officer."

Now came the final part of our unique trip.

Initially I felt rather ill at ease, because I was afraid we would have troubles with the tires again, but after a while the beauty of this part of the country erased all my worries.

The road from Franzensbad to Plauen leads through one of the loveliest countrysides I have known. Everything was dipped in golden afternoon sunshine, and we both savoured this particular part of our drive. The cordial hospitality in Franzensbad, followed by a ride in warm sunshine, the fresh air fraught with the scent of fir resin, and most of all the intense awareness of freedom, greatly offset the uncomfortable ride with rucksack and missing pillion accessories.

The ruins of levelled Plauen were a terrible sight and a bitter contrast to the peaceful, almost untouched nature we had just driven through.

Surprisingly, Friedl and her parents had already prepared everything for our return that day.

'How is that possible?' one may ask.

At times, Friedl's mother had certain, unexplainable premonitions which turned out to come true. In the morning of that very day, for instance, she maintained stubbornly that we would arrive in the evening on the motorcycle. Even after curfew, when everybody else had given up hope for that day, she insisted we would still come. Fifteen minutes after the beginning of curfew, the two of us drove up.

For the first time, my mother embraced her daughter-in-law, and a bad chapter in her life came to a good end. In fact, this chapter would have ended with death in a gas chamber had not some bureaucrat in Theresienstadt made a mistake by omitting to register two of the people from the former Plauen-transport for deportation to Auschwitz. Thank God!

ANNOTATIONS

[1] Loewenstein, Karl. "Minsk — Im Lager der deutschen Juden" (In the Camp of the German Jews). Heft 51. Bonn: Bundeszentrale für Heimatdienst, 1961.

[2] Heydecker, Joe & Leeb, Johannes. "Der Nürnberger Prozess" (The Nuremberg Trials). Köln-Frankfurt a.M.: Kiepenheuer & Witsch, 1981.

[3] Davidowicz, Lucy S. "The War Against the Jews, 1933-1945". New York, N.Y.: Holt, Rinehart and Winston, 1979.

[4] Onkel Otto, who was murdered by the Nazis in Minsk, and Little-Omi (Klein-Omi), who perished in the concentration camp Theresienstadt, were not the only ones of the family who died by the hand of Hitler's killer gangs. Many of our relatives in Poland disappeared without a trace at the time of the German occupation when there was no more chance to emigrate or escape. Jews were kidnapped straight from their homes or on the streets, and often even the closest members of a family did not know the whereabouts of a spouse, child or parent.

While the tragic fates of most of my relatives who lived in Poland are still buried under a pile of big question-marks, my investigations reveal with certainty only what happened to six of them:

a. Barbara Fuhrmann, née Toeplitz, was killed by the Germans in Galicia, where she went searching for her husband Jan, who was a captain with the Polish Army and senior orderly officer of General Sikorski, hoping to find him there. He had been kidnapped and †deported by the Soviets and killed in the massacre of Katyn.

b. Withold Luxemburg was arrested and killed by the Germans in Vilna, Lithuania.

c. Jan Meyer was arrested and killed by the Germans.

d. Artur Toeplitz was killed during the Warsaw Ghetto Uprising in 1943.

e. Henryk Toeplitz was murdered by the Germans in 1941 or

1943 (two different sources of information - the more likely date is 1941).

f. Karol Wellisch was arrested by the Germans during the occupation (no year available) and disappeared.

[5] Mrs. Selma Simon was the wife of the president of the Jewish Community in Plauen, Adolf Simon, who passed away on July 23rd, 1925, at the age of 60, because of a heart ailment. Upon his death Mrs. Simon established the "Adolf Simon Foundation."

[6] Adler, Dr. H.G. — "Theresienstadt". Tübingen: J.C.B.Mohr (Paul Siebeck), 1960.

[7] During the existence of Theresienstadt (Terezín) as a concentration camp, there were three commandants: Burger, Rahm and Seidl

a. SS-Hauptsturmführer Siegfried Seidl (commandant from December 1941 to July 3rd, 1943) was sentenced to death by an Austrian court in 1946.

b. SS-Obersturmführer Anton Burger took over the command of KZ Theresienstadt from S. Seidl on July 3rd, 1943. He was later replaced by Rahm. According to documents, the former then played an active role in the persecution and rounding up of Jews in Greece, particularly the Greek island of Corfu. Information received from the Zentrale Stelle der Landesjustizverwaltungen, (Central Authority of the Justice Administrations of (German) States), Ludwigsburg, confirms that Burger was arrested after the war with the intent to extradite him to the CSR. However, Burger escaped and has not been found since. This was also confirmed by YAD VASHEM, Jerusalem, and the Simon Wiesenthal Center, Los Angeles. He was sentenced to death in absentia by the Special Peoples Court, Leitmeritz, CSR. [YAD VASHEM in Jerusalem is an archive and the memorial centre for Jews killed by the Nazis.]

It may not be too far fetched to believe that Burger either found haven in South America and lives (lived?) a comfortable life there, protected by the organization of former SS comrades, or lives (lived?) in an Arab country like the Jew-murderer and Eichmann's right-hand man, Alois Brunner.

c. SS-Obersturmführer Karl Rahm (commandant from February 8th, 1944, to May 5th, 1945, at which time he disappeared from Theresienstadt) was found, put on trial in the CSR in 1947, sentenced to death and executed (Special Peoples Court Leitmeritz).

[8] Kogon, Eugen "Der SS-Staat" Munich, Wilhelm Heine Verlag, 1992. English title: "The Theory and Practice of Hell."

[9] My sister, Inge, worked as accountant and secretary in a wholesale seed company. As they supplied farmers with seeds, they were classified by the Nazi government as "strategically essential" for the war effort. Inge had a very decent employer, who always claimed that he could not release her for slave labour since he was lacking reliable personnel already, and he would be unable to replace Inge with an equally qualified person. With such protection she was saved from ghetto houses, labour camps and maybe worse.

After Germany occupied the Netherlands, Corri was deported to Germany for slave labour. He wound up in an open foreign labour camp in our hometown where he had to work in the field of cabinet making and carpentry for the Junkers Aircraft company. He was not trained in these professions but, since he was very handy, the Germans decided that was what he had to do. After several months, he was able to improve his situation a little and helping his comrades at the same time by being an interpreter on occasions. By then, he had already a good command of the German language.

His working place was next to the house where Inge had her flat. One day, when Corri and his fellow workers had a break, Inge saw them all drinking from one cup and felt sorry for them, so she went and bought several cups, put cigarettes and cookies in each and gave these to the chaps. As a "delegate", Corri went and thanked Inge, in the name of all of the labourers, for her kindness. And that was how they met.

There were no mail, phone or transport connections during that time, as already mentioned, and, therefore, we could not notify each other about our wedding dates. It turned out that we married not only on exactly the same day but almost at the same time.

[10] I reported about this newsreel in my letter to Dr. H.G. Adler, dated July 26th, 1957, and he in turn mentioned it in his book "Theresienstadt" (2nd edition), page 184. Tübingen: J.C.B. Mohr (Paul Siebeck), 1960, as well as in his other book "Die verheimlichte Wahrheit" (The Concealed Truth), page 324. Tübingen:

J.C.B. Mohr (Paul Siebeck), 1958.

[11] Not knowing for which purpose the Caserne Mortier, Paris, was used after the war, I decided to visit this place in May 1986, and found out that the complex is once more a French military installation, as it was originally. Vis-à-vis from the Caserne Mortier is now the Department of National Defence. For this reason, I did not want to take pictures without official permission, not even outside.

After explaining at length to several barrack guards the purpose of my visit, Friedl and I were finally taken to the Commander of the Caserne Mortier, Chef d'Escadron G. Roger, and a security officer. With their kind consent, I was allowed to take a picture of the building into which we had been crammed as prisoners before being transported to Valognes in April 1944. Commander Roger also permitted me to photograph the yard, where we experienced so many roll-calls under SS-Obersturmführer Müller after our deportation from Saxony. Somehow, it was an emotional moment seeing the Tricolore proudly flying in the sunshine over the gate.

[12] The gentleman who had supplied me with maps and charts and generously invited Friedl and me to stay at their castle during our visit to the Valognes area is Monsieur René Le Doux, master of the Château de Chiffrevast, Tamerville.

Incidentally, this huge and impressive castle had been rebuilt as early as the beginning of the 17th century, after an original construction in the 11th century and a later destruction.

Not only was Monsieur Le Doux extremely helpful in driving me around in my efforts locating and identifying certain places I got to know in 1944 (nolens-volens), but his, and his wife's, warm hospitality cannot be praised enough. He insisted, I should "return home with better memories from Normandy than the first time." Madame Jacqueline Le Doux, by the way, is not only a great expert on fine arts, but also a very talented restorer of old oil-paintings. -

[13] When we arrived at the now rebuilt Valognes (May/June 1986), I had the opportunity to take pictures of the Ecole Ste. Marie as the Pensionnat de Jeunes Filles is called nowadays. The entrance, the staircase to the gallery, and "our room" all still exist except for

the twenty-five narrow bunkbeds used in this room in 1944. Now there were seven regular beds. The old buildings surrounding the courtyard in horseshoe-fashion are still standing as they did in 1944, but modern structures have been added adjacent to the two old wings.

[14] A journalist from the daily, "La Presse de la Manche", Cherbourg, interviewed us in Monsieur Le Doux' castle, and a three-quarter page article appeared the next day in that paper.

Shortly after, Monsieur Le Doux met a man who had read the article and had worked in a bakery across the street from our prison-camp in those days. He remembered having seen us in our miserable condition. Another man told Monsieur Le Doux, he was the third Frenchman, together with Monsieur Cornat, the late mayor of Valognes, and another man, who participated with Alfred and myself in the rescue effort to free Mademoiselle Brochard from under the ruins, where she was trapped. Monsieur Le Doux, who at the time of the Invasion was in charge of a Red Cross team, experienced many extraordinary situations himself during that turbulent epoch.

[15] With Monsieur Le Doux' help I obtained an interesting book, "Constructions Spéciales" by Roland Hautefeuille. With the valuable information contained in this book, I was able to ascertain that the construction site we had been working on must have been COUVILLE.

Up to that moment, I was not sure to which of several places we had been driven under guard in those days, although I could safely eliminate two of the four German construction sites on the Cotentin peninsula, judging from how long it took the trucks to get us there in '44.

This left me with Sottevast and Couville. During our "inspection tours," we found that vegetation had grown everywhere over the remains of the rocket launching sites, under construction during the war. Although the terrain at Couville, with its parallel ramps, appeared to be most probably our old workplace, I had no definite proof until I read this book "Constructions Spéciales" which confirmed my presumption. The Couville site, referred to by the Germans as B.8, or Structure 8, was the only active site on Cotentin controlled by the Luftwaffe (German Air Force,) and I always recalled that our construction site passes had been issued by the Luftwaffen-Baukommando (Air-Force Construction Department). Sottevast/Brix, on the other hand, had always been under the jurisdiction of the Heer (army).

It is very significant that documents received from the German Federal Archives prove that the OT-Oberbauleitung (OT Chief Construction Management) Cherbourg had a special department for "Cooperation with the SS Liaison Command" (SS-Verbindungsführung).

[16] With dwindling construction supplies and constant destruction by bombs, the launching site structures became less and less rugged, as we had to rebuild and rebuild them.

By far the greatest damage to B.8 was caused during an air raid by the 9th US Air Force on November 11th, 1943. It must be pointed out, however, that this attack was only carried out after a serious warning requesting all workers as well as the population to leave this region.

As it appears at present, supply shortages may not have been the sole reason for the gradual reduction of structures in quality and quantity. General Heinemann, commander of the LXV German Army Corps, had noted that certain construction goals could not be met because of Allied air superiority yet, for reasons of deception, some construction work at Couville was ordered to be carried on.

Apart from attacks on Couville before 1944, the tables in "Constructions Speciales" mention one in which flying fortresses dropped twenty-five tons of bombs on this relatively small area (April 27th, 1944) and one in which Boston bombers dropped 17 tons of bombs (May 12th, 1944). This writer believes, however, there must have been at least one or two more air raids on our construction site between April and D-Day than indicated.

Couville fell into the hands of the Americans on June 21st, 1944, i.e. fifteen days after the Landing.

[17] Corri, now my brother-in-law, told me how he obtained the addresses of the underground contacts. When German troops violated every international law by blitz-attacks on France, Belgium and the Netherlands in May 1940, the Nazis tried to eliminate every

possible source of military resistance as well as political opposition. From here on, Dutch people began helping their countrymen who were in danger. These early actions were by no means organized but person-to-person matters. Later, when the Germans had established their occupation forces and oppressed and persecuted the Dutch civilians on a large scale, most Dutch people became so infuriated about the brutalities of the foreign power that they organized in the Underground. What had been, initially, simply aid groups gradually consolidated to sizable underground movements. A friend of Corri's who was part of such an organized group gave him the contact addresses of these underground cells immediately after learning that Corri himself was on the deportation list for Germany as a slave labourer. Then, after Corri learned that I would be sent on a "transport", he gave me these addresses, too, hoping that one day I could make my escape and use them.

[18] Monsieur Le Doux, very active with the Red Cross during the Débarquement, mentioned that the reason for the Allied airplanes coming over Valognes in large waves *with all their lights on* was that they were on a visual flightcourse in extremely close formation during the night from the 5th to the 6th of June, 1944. Without the lights on, they could have easily rammed each other, particularly when manoeuvering to avoid the German AAD (antiaircraft defence). On the other hand, the illuminated Allied planes must have been easier targets for the Germans.

[19] Mademoiselle Brochard is alive, at the time of this writing, and as well as can be expected. She owned a bookshop in a barrack at the time I met her in 1952. She retired after she occupied a shop in one of the nice, rebuilt houses in Valognes. Unfortunately, she was away on vacation when we were in town in 1986.

[20] Monsieur Le Doux helped us in trying to determine the location of the farmhouse and barn in which we settled after Otf. Leutner's order to vacate the Pensionnat de Jeunes Filles and to leave Valognes proper. It seems that both buildings disappeared with the construction of the modern highway to Cherbourg.

[21] I believe, the farmhouse near the place where we had buried the Gypsy comrade still exists. In my estimation, it must be close to the intersection of Routc National #13 and La Petite Route.

Little time and bad weather did not permit a thorough investigation into the sad circumstances of the final resting place of our compañero during the 1986 visit to Valognes but I shall examine the matter further at some future time.

[22] One may be surprised that, in my writing, I did not mention the British and Canadian war efforts and participation in the Invasion, because there is a lot to be said about this chapter of history too. It is not my intent to minimize these enormous contributions in material and even more in lost lives and health. Considering my topic, I restricted myself to giving an account of the events happening in the region around our camp and construction site. This meant focussing on US operations near Valognes and the Utah Beach area, and not describing D-Day, Operation Overlord and the Débarquement in general. Dealing with the latter events in this context would have simply been repetitive, as these historic facts are well known and vastly documented.

[23] During our interesting trip through Normandy in 1986, I was able to take pictures of the Abbaye Blanche in Mortain where Alfred and I had worked in the German field hospital for free bed and meals. I took additional photos of the railroad crossing at Domfront. Unfortunately, because of weather conditions, the photos do not lend themselves to good reproduction.

The hollow way into which Alfred and I had catapulted ourselves seconds after we heard the bombers coming down for an attack is not hollow anymore. With the construction of a hospital on its westside, the slope which made it a "hollow" way was levelled.

The destroyed Domfront has been rebuilt into a beautiful town, once again reflecting its ancient character.

As Alfred and I were seeking protection from debris flying through the air, caused by the pattern bombing of Domfront, we threw ourselves behind a hedge near a farmhouse. I found the road on the hill but was unable to identify the farmhouse and the hedge. Both of them may not exist anymore.

[24] At one point Alfred and I ran into a trap of Army/OT control between Alençon and Mamers and were taken by a guard to an OT camp in the forest. On our trip, I could make out the wooded area but stopped searching for the one-time camp, or for the exact

location where the camp had been, due to the incessant, pouring rain.

On a sunny day, I would have even searched for the place where we had eaten the wild strawberries in '44.

[25] It was sunny when we came to the location where the former German airfield outside of Chartres must have been. However, nothing, but absolutely nothing, resembled the terrain as I remembered it. The land is now completely built up with houses, hangars, terminal building and control tower. Moreover, what is now Chartres' regular airport is surrounded by an almost confusing network of roads.

[26] It was really saddening to see the mansion of Coltainville in its 1986 state. What had once been a charming country seat amidst a beautiful little park was now an agglomeration of decaying walls under a broken roof. The wooden shutters, typical for houses in the French countryside, nearly fell from their hinges. It needed major repairs to become habitable again.

In 1994, the administrative building and an annex had been perfectly renovated and the three-sectioned main-building was in its first stage of renovation.

[27] As mentioned, we were miraculously saved from execution through the Nazi Feldgendarmerie by a Lieutenant of the German air force. I visited this place three times after the war. In 1972 my cousin Georges had driven us there. Twice I recognized the field at the bend of the road near the S.C.A.R. Ablis silo (I had always mistaken it for a flour-mill.), and the old railway station with the sign "Paray-Douaville." But why does the piece of field carry such memories? For indefinable reasons it is more engraved in my mind than the part of the road on which everything happened. This parcel of land also disappeared and made way for an expressway overpass.

[28] From the many visits throughout the years we know Paris is Paris once more, with all the advantages and disadvantages of a metropolis. On the occasion of our last visit we were amazed by the great improvement of the Métro system, specifically the Métro stations which are much cleaner than years ago. The Métro always had a specific smell. Being in such a Métro station with closed eyes, one could always tell one was in Paris. Fortunately (for me), some

of this indefinable yet unique odour of the olden days still lingers.

Paris with swastika flags flying over the Champs Elysées and streets echoing the sound of German soldiers and SS boots was just not Paris. Paris then was a city sick with visible boils and festering ulcers. The blood red swastika flags merely documented that situation. As far as I am concerned, Paris, being ashamed of her disfigurement, went into hiding after the occupation, May 14th, 1940, till the end of August 1944 when it was liberated.

[29] Alfred Eisenhardt was a very reliable companion in the prison camp and even much more so later during our escape. However, all my attempts to locate him after the war failed.

[30] No exact information could be extracted from any source on the whereabouts of Dog-Whip-Arnold. According to whisperings, he lived in the resort town of Sonneberg, Thuringia, then East Germany, where he was said to have owned a house. Hearsay has it, this former Gestapo functionary had been "turned around" by the Soviets and afterwards by the East German authorities who both used him as an informer. From what I learned in secret, he was regularly sent to the Leipzig Fairs to spy on visitors from the West.

[31] The case of Albert Agsten is significant in itself and as a post-war incident typical of the West German denazification and legal procedures. Altogether, it is a deplorable story.

The reader has been already familiarized with A. Agsten in the earlier text. Agsten was in charge of a Gestapo district office (Zwickau) in Saxony, Germany. The first time I met him was in 1942 when he and Arnold searched my mother's apartment and behaved like madmen.

Police files show that he was responsible for the death of 168 Dutch and Belgian slave labourers. He brutalized prisoners as he did this writer in his Gestapo office two months before the war ended. After he had me beaten up, he sent me to prison for later transport to the Flossenbürg Concentration Camp. Incidentally, the head of the "Führer's" military counterespionage, Admiral Wilhelm Canaris, was executed by Hitler's order in this very same KZ in April 1945, the month our transfer had been set.

Somehow, Agsten escaped from the Soviet occupied territory and lived in the British Zone of Germany after the war. Maybe one of the Anglo-allied intelligence services believed he would be an anti-Soviet asset, just as Klaus Barbie, the Butcher of Lyon, had been on the CIC payroll.

I was the only witness at his denazification trial in Kassel, when my testimony was to the greatest extent ignored by the chairmen of the tribunal. The trial took place in the last phase of the denazification period in Germany and Agsten got away with a ridiculously light sentence and no detention.

In February 1949, I filed charges against Agsten with the criminal courts in Germany. When I had not heard from the courts for over three years, I contacted them and was informed that charges were suspended because of the Law Regarding Immunity from Criminal Prosecution. This court decision, however, had already been made fourteen months after I had brought suit against Agsten but I, the plaintiff, had neither been called as witness, nor been notified about the court's ruling!

The murder of 168 slave labourers and the mistreatment of prisoners had simply been swept under the rug; these matters had not even been included in the charges by the court. The court had ruled that the short, temporary political internment of Agsten had been considered in the judgement as part of a confinement this chief of the Gestapo would have had to expect for battery and assault. The remainder of the calculated period of detention would then fall under the law already mentioned.

Agsten should have been charged with war-crimes.

At the trial, Agsten declared that he was *forced* to join the Secret State Police! The court must have known quite well that this statement was a total fabrication. Nobody would have been *drafted* to the Secret Police, let alone forced to advance in the ranks for the position of head of a district.

The type of person Agsten was is also shown by a statement from his former secretary. She declared that Agsten once left his office with a rubber truncheon to interrogate prisoners. He returned, stained with blood and cursing. He had "pumped" the prisoners for information with savage mercilessness.

It remains a sad fact that many Nazis could evade justice, because, after the war, German courts were still staffed with old-guard Nazi lawyers, who did not pass harsh sentences against Nazi criminals for their activities during the "Third Reich".

[32] Forty years after my liberation from prison, and on its actual anniversary, I was sitting in a fine Montréal restaurant, together with my wife and our two married daughters, celebrating my survival and, therefore, the subsequent existence of our children and grandchildren.

My choice of where to go after gaining freedom had brought me back to the girl I loved, the daughter of the people who had hidden me after I had escaped from the forced labour camp in occupied France.

Table of Contents

INTRODUCTION 9

PART ONE

I. KLEIN — OMI. 13
II. NAZI LEGISLATION (ANTI-JEWISH DECREES) 16
III. THE BEGINNING OF THE WAR — GHETTO HOUSES 27
IV. MY GRANDMOTHER AND THERESIENSTADT. . . . 33
    My Visit to Theresienstadt 36

V. MY MOTHER AND THERESIENSTADT (TEREZÍN) . . 44
    1. In the Theresienstadt Camp 51
    2. The Beautification Hoax 57
    3. The Last Months in Theresienstadt. 61

VI. OCCUPIED FRANCE 64
    1. Valognes 67
    2. Marching Through Valognes 77
    3. At the Atlantic Wall 80
    4. Will There be an Invasion? 84
    5. The Invasion 86
    6. Background Information 99
    7. The Escape 104
    8. Paris 126

VII. BACK IN GERMANY

    In the First Months of 1945 133

PART TWO

VIII. AFTER THE LIBERATION
   1. Back to the right to live................... 151
   2. The US Counter Intelligence Corps 154
   3. Wedding Obstacles...................... 157

IX. A MOTHER COMES HOME 162

ANNOTATIONS 179